Nicaragua
Travel Guide

The Complete Guide to Discover, Embark and Experience the Best of Nicaragua's Natural Beauty, Rich Culture and Vibrant History

Juliet Bryan

Dedication

This book is dedicated to those captivated by the vibrant spirit of Nicaragua. May it be your trusted companion, guiding you through remarkable journey in the cities of Nicaragua.

Table of Contents

Preface

Welcome to the captivating realm of the "Nicaragua Travel Guide: The Complete Guide to Discover, Embark and Experience the Best of Nicaragua's Natural Beauty, Rich Culture, and Vibrant History." Within these pages lies your passport to a journey like no other – an odyssey that will transport you through the heart of Nicaragua's diverse landscapes, centuries-old heritage, and the warmth of its people.

As you embark on this immersive expedition, allow me to be your compass, guiding you through the enchanting landscapes, bustling cities, and tranquil havens that define Nicaragua. This guide is meticulously crafted to provide you not only with practical insights but also to infuse your journey with the essence of Nicaragua's vibrant culture.

Whether you're a thrill-seeking adventurer, an avid cultural explorer or a family seeking unforgettable experiences, this guide is designed to cater to your unique travel aspirations. Dive into detailed itineraries that lead you through the heart of each region, uncovering the hidden gems, historical landmarks, and natural wonders that make Nicaragua a true gem of Central America.

Beyond the surface, I delve into the intricacies of local customs, introduce you to essential Spanish phrases, and provide you with insider tips that will empower you to connect deeply with Nicaragua's soul. I invite you to embrace the flavors of traditional cuisine, engage with the vibrancy of local markets, and immerse yourself in the tales of Nicaragua's past and present.

As you hold this guide in your hands, you are holding more than just a collection of pages – you are holding the key to an unforgettable journey. Let the "Nicaragua Travel Guide" be your constant companion, opening doors to breathtaking landscapes, enriching encounters, and memories that will last a lifetime. It's time to embark on the journey of discovery and embrace the undeniable beauty of Nicaragua.

1

Introduction

Nicaragua, officially known as the Republic of Nicaragua, is a captivating Central American country located between the Pacific Ocean and the Caribbean Sea. With its rich history, stunning landscapes, and vibrant culture, Nicaragua has become an increasingly popular destination for travelers seeking an authentic and diverse experience. This travel guide aims to provide comprehensive information to help you explore and make the most of your journey through this fascinating country.

About Nicaragua

Nicaragua boasts a history that dates back to ancient times when indigenous civilizations inhabited the region. It was later colonized by the Spanish in the 16th century, leaving behind a remarkable blend of indigenous and colonial influences that shape the country's identity.

Today, Nicaragua is known for its warm hospitality and friendly locals. Spanish is the official language, and the predominant religion is Roman Catholicism, which plays a significant role in shaping the nation's culture and traditions.

The country's economy is diverse, relying on industries like agriculture, mining, tourism, and manufacturing. Coffee and bananas are among the major agricultural exports, contributing to the nation's economy and cultural heritage.

1

Geographical Overview

Nicaragua is blessed with natural wonders, making it a paradise for nature lovers and adventure seekers alike. The country's topography includes a mix of mountains, volcanoes, lakes, rivers, and pristine beaches, creating a captivating landscape that leaves travelers in awe.

The Central American nation is bordered by Honduras to the north and Costa Rica to the south. It covers an area of approximately 130,373 square kilometers (50,336 square miles). Its unique geographical location places it in the heart of the isthmus connecting North and South America, and it plays a vital role in both regional and global ecosystems.

Mountains and Volcanoes

Nicaragua is part of the Ring of Fire, a region with a high concentration of volcanic activity along the Pacific Ocean. The country is home to over 19 volcanoes, some of which are still active. One of the most famous is Momotombo, a symmetrical stratovolcano that stands proudly along the shores of Lake Managua.

Lakes and Rivers

The largest freshwater lake in Central America, Lake Nicaragua (also known as Lake Cocibolca), dominates the southwestern region of the country. The lake's picturesque beauty is enhanced by the presence of the enchanting volcanic Ometepe Island, formed by two volcanoes rising from the water's surface.

Nicaragua also boasts several other lakes and rivers, providing ample opportunities for water-based activities such as fishing, kayaking, and boat tours.

The Pacific and Caribbean Coasts

With a coastline stretching over 910 kilometers (566 miles), Nicaragua offers diverse coastal landscapes. The Pacific coast features stunning beaches with opportunities for surfing and relaxation, while the Caribbean coast offers a more laid-back atmosphere with a rich Afro-Caribbean cultural influence.

Climate and Weather

Nicaragua's geographical diversity plays a significant role in shaping its climate and weather patterns. The country experiences a tropical climate, which is influenced by both the Pacific Ocean to the west and the Caribbean Sea to the east. The differences in altitude across the landscape contribute to varying microclimates, making Nicaragua an intriguing destination with distinct weather conditions.

Dry Season and Rainy Season

Nicaragua has two main seasons - the dry season and the rainy season, also known as the wet season. Understanding the characteristics of each season is crucial for planning your trip and ensuring you make the most of your experience.

Dry Season (December to April)

- The dry season is considered the high tourist season in Nicaragua and for good reason. It is characterized by clear skies, warm temperatures, and minimal rainfall, making it an ideal time for outdoor activities and exploration.

- Temperatures during the dry season typically range from 25°C to 30°C (77°F to 86°F) in the lowlands, while the highlands enjoy a more moderate climate with temperatures ranging from 15°C to 25°C (59°F to 77°F).
- The lack of rain during this period ensures better road conditions, making travel and sightseeing more accessible.
- Popular destinations like Granada, San Juan del Sur, and Ometepe Island see an influx of tourists during the dry season, so it's advisable to book accommodations and tours in advance.
- Rainy Season (May to November):
- The rainy season in Nicaragua brings a refreshing change to the landscape as the countryside transforms into lush greenery. The rains usually arrive in the afternoon or evening and are often accompanied by thunderstorms.
- While the rainy season might deter some travelers, it also presents unique opportunities to witness Nicaragua's natural beauty at its peak. The landscapes come alive with vibrant colors, and the flora and fauna thrive.
- The Caribbean coast experiences more rainfall throughout the year, and the intensity of rains may vary depending on the region.
- The advantage of traveling during the rainy season is fewer crowds and lower accommodation prices. Additionally, some outdoor activities, like rafting and birdwatching, are even more rewarding during this time.

Microclimates

Nicaragua's diverse topography results in microclimates, where weather conditions can vary significantly in small geographical areas. For example, the central highlands, including cities like Matagalpa and Estelí, tend to be cooler due to higher elevations. On the other hand, coastal areas like San Juan del Sur and Leon are generally warmer, especially during the dry season.

Hurricane Season

It's essential to be aware of the hurricane season, which occurs in the Atlantic basin from June to November. While Nicaragua's Pacific coast is less prone to direct hurricane impacts, the Caribbean coast is more vulnerable. During this time, it's crucial to monitor weather updates and heed any advisories issued by local authorities.

Packing Tips

When planning a trip to Nicaragua, it's essential to pack for the specific season you'll be visiting. For the dry season, lightweight clothing, sunscreen, a wide-brimmed hat, and sunglasses are recommended. If you're traveling during the rainy season, pack lightweight rain gear, sturdy footwear, and quick-drying clothing. Mosquito repellent is also essential, especially in areas with higher humidity. Introduction

Nicaragua, officially known as the Republic of Nicaragua, is a captivating Central American country located between the Pacific Ocean and the Caribbean Sea. With its rich history, stunning landscapes, and vibrant culture, Nicaragua has become an increasingly popular destination for travelers seeking an authentic and diverse experience. This travel guide aims to provide comprehensive information to help you explore and make the most of your journey through this fascinating country.

Cultural Background of Nicaragua

The cultural background of Nicaragua is a fascinating tapestry woven from a rich blend of indigenous heritage, Spanish colonial influence, African roots, and modern-day traditions. Understanding the cultural fabric of this Central American nation is key to appreciating its people, customs, and way of life. In this section, we'll delve deep into the various aspects that contribute to Nicaragua's unique cultural identity.

Indigenous Roots

Before the arrival of the Spanish, Nicaragua was inhabited by various indigenous tribes, each with its distinct language, traditions, and art. Some of the prominent indigenous groups included the Miskito, Sumo, Rama, and Chorotega peoples. These indigenous communities were skilled in agriculture, fishing, and crafting intricate ceramics and textiles.

Despite the impact of colonization and modernization, many indigenous customs and practices persist today, especially in remote regions of the country. Efforts are being made to preserve and revitalize indigenous languages and cultural heritage, recognizing their significant contribution to Nicaragua's identity.

Spanish Colonial Influence

Nicaragua's cultural landscape was profoundly shaped by Spanish colonization, which began in the early 16th century. The Spanish brought their language, religion, and architectural style, leaving a lasting imprint on the country.

Language: Spanish is the official language of Nicaragua, and it is widely spoken across the country. However, in some rural areas, indigenous languages and Creole languages are still spoken, showcasing the country's linguistic diversity.

Religion: The influence of Spanish colonialism is most evident in Nicaragua's predominant religion - Roman Catholicism. The Catholic Church played a crucial role in shaping the cultural and social fabric of the nation. Religious festivities and traditions are deeply ingrained in Nicaraguan society, with religious processions, fiestas, and patron saint celebrations being prominent throughout the year.

Colonial Architecture: The legacy of Spanish colonial architecture can be witnessed in cities like Granada and Leon. These cities boast well-preserved colonial buildings, including churches, cathedrals, and plazas, showcasing the intricate designs and craftsmanship of that era.

Afro-Caribbean Influence

Nicaragua's Caribbean coast is home to a vibrant Afro-Caribbean culture, predominantly influenced by the descendants of African slaves who were brought to the region during colonial times. The culture in this area is distinct from the rest of Nicaragua, featuring its dialects, music, dance, and culinary traditions.

Language and Dialects: The Creole language, also known as Miskito Coast Creole or Coastal Creole English, is spoken by many Afro-Caribbean communities on the Caribbean coast. It is a

7

unique blend of English, Spanish, and indigenous languages, reflecting the multicultural history of the region.

Music and Dance: Afro-Caribbean music, such as Palo de Mayo and Reggae, is an integral part of the cultural heritage in this region. The vibrant rhythms and colorful dance performances are deeply rooted in African traditions and are a captivating sight during local celebrations and festivals.

Gastronomy: The cuisine on Nicaragua's Caribbean coast is known for its rich flavors and use of coconut, seafood, and tropical fruits. Dishes like Rondon, a hearty coconut-based stew with fish and root vegetables, are iconic to the region.

Modern-Day Traditions

As Nicaragua embraces modernization, it has managed to retain many cherished traditions and customs that have been passed down through generations.

Festivals and Celebrations: Nicaragua is known for its lively festivals, where communities come together to celebrate their cultural heritage. From the colorful Semana Santa (Holy Week) processions to the vibrant Fiestas Patronales (Patron Saint Festivals), these events offer a glimpse into the country's deeply rooted religious and cultural beliefs.

Art and Handicrafts: Artisanal crafts, such as pottery, woodcarving, and weaving, are an essential part of Nicaragua's cultural expression. Artisans create intricate designs and motifs that reflect the country's natural beauty and diverse cultural influences.

Music and Dance: Nicaragua's music scene is a vibrant mix of traditional folk music, popular Latin genres, and modern urban styles. Traditional marimba music and dance performances are a delight to experience, as they represent the soul of Nicaraguan culture.

Gastronomy: Nicaraguan cuisine is a fusion of indigenous, Spanish, and Afro-Caribbean influences, resulting in a diverse and flavorful gastronomic experience. Local dishes like gallo pinto (rice and beans), vigorón (yucca and pork salad), and nacatamal (similar to a tamale) are staples that showcase the country's culinary heritage.

Family and Community: Family values and close-knit communities play a significant role in Nicaraguan society. Family gatherings and social events are essential occasions for strengthening bonds and preserving cultural traditions.

Literature and Art: Nicaragua has a rich literary and artistic heritage, with renowned poets, writers, and painters contributing to the nation's cultural tapestry. Artists like Rubén Darío, the father of modernist poetry, have left an indelible mark on the world of literature.

As you embark on this adventure, let the spirit of exploration guide you to uncover the hidden treasures and authentic experiences that await in this Central American treasure, leaving you with cherished memories of a truly exceptional travel experience.

2

Preparing for Your Trip

Planning a trip to Nicaragua requires careful preparation to ensure a smooth and enjoyable experience. From understanding entry requirements to organizing your itinerary and packing essentials, this section will provide you with comprehensive travel planning tips to make the most of your adventure in this Central American gem.

Travel Planning Tips

Research and Itinerary

- Begin your travel planning by researching Nicaragua's top destinations, attractions, and activities. Decide on the regions you want to explore and create a rough itinerary to help you organize your trip efficiently.
- Consider the time of year you'll be visiting to tailor your itinerary around the weather conditions and local festivals.

Entry Requirements

- Check the visa requirements for your nationality before traveling to Nicaragua. Citizens from many countries, including the United States, Canada, and the European Union, can enter Nicaragua visa-free for a specified period.

10

- Ensure your passport is valid for at least six months beyond your planned departure date.

Health and Vaccinations

- Consult a travel health professional or visit a travel clinic to get advice on recommended vaccinations and health precautions for Nicaragua.
- Common vaccines for Nicaragua may include Hepatitis A and B, typhoid, and routine vaccinations.

Travel Insurance

- Purchase comprehensive travel insurance that covers medical emergencies, trip cancellations, and other unforeseen circumstances.
- Make sure the insurance policy includes coverage for adventure activities if you plan to engage in any high-risk sports.

Budgeting and Currency

- Create a budget for your trip to Nicaragua, taking into account expenses for accommodation, meals, transportation, activities, and souvenirs.
- Nicaragua's official currency is the Nicaraguan Cordoba (NIO). While credit cards are widely accepted in major cities, it's advisable to carry some cash, especially when traveling to more remote areas.

Language

- While Spanish is the official language, learning a few basic Spanish phrases can greatly enhance your travel experience and interactions with the locals.

Accommodation and Transportation

- Book your accommodation in advance, especially if you're traveling during the peak tourist season (dry season).
- Consider various transportation options, including domestic flights, buses, and private shuttles, to move between different regions of Nicaragua.

Safety and Security

- Nicaragua is generally safe for tourists, but it's essential to exercise caution and be aware of your surroundings, especially in urban areas.
- Avoid displaying expensive items and valuables in public and use hotel safes for storing passports and important documents.

Responsible Travel

- Embrace responsible and sustainable travel practices during your trip to minimize your impact on the environment and support local communities.
- Choose eco-friendly accommodations and tour operators that prioritize environmental conservation and responsible tourism practices.

Electrical Adapters

- Nicaragua uses type A and type B electrical outlets, with a standard voltage of 120 V and a frequency of 60 Hz. Don't forget to come
- with appropriate adapters for your electronic devices.

Communication and Internet

- Nicaraguan mobile networks provide good coverage in most urban areas. Consider purchasing a local SIM card for data and calls during your stay.
- Many hotels, cafes, and restaurants offer free Wi-Fi but keep in mind that the connection speed might vary in remote regions.

Emergency Contacts

- Save essential emergency contacts, including your country's embassy or consulate, local emergency services, and your travel insurance provider.

Pack Light and Smart

- Nicaragua's climate is generally warm, so pack lightweight, breathable clothing. However, if you plan to visit higher altitudes, bring some warmer layers.
- Pack comfortable footwear for exploring various terrains, such as walking shoes or sandals for city excursions and sturdy hiking boots for nature adventures.
- Don't forget essentials like sunscreen, insect repellent, a hat, sunglasses, and a reusable water bottle to stay hydrated.

13

Learn About Local Customs

- Familiarize yourself with local customs and cultural norms to show respect to the local population. Greetings, gestures, and appropriate clothing can vary across regions and communities.

Stay Flexible

- Embrace the laid-back pace of Nicaragua and be open to unexpected experiences. It's okay to adjust your plans if you stumble upon hidden gems along the way.

By following these travel planning tips, you'll be well-prepared to embark on an unforgettable journey through Nicaragua. From the moment you step foot in this captivating country to the last days of your adventure, you'll be immersed in the beauty of its landscapes, charmed by the warmth of its people, and captivated by its vibrant cultural heritage. Prepare to create memories that will last a lifetime as you explore the diverse landscapes, soak in the cultural richness, and uncover the hidden treasures of this extraordinary Central American destination.

Visa and Entry Requirements for Nicaragua

Traveling to Nicaragua requires understanding the visa and entry requirements set by the country's immigration authorities. These regulations vary based on your nationality and the purpose of your visit. In this comprehensive guide, we will explore the different visa types, visa exemptions, and essential entry requirements to ensure a smooth and hassle-free journey to this enchanting Central American nation.

Visa Types for Nicaragua

Tourist Visa (Entry Visa)

- The tourist visa is the most common type of visa for travelers visiting Nicaragua for leisure, sightseeing, and exploration.
- Depending on your nationality, you may be eligible for a visa waiver or may need to apply for a tourist visa in advance from a Nicaraguan consulate or embassy.

Business Visa

- The business visa is for travelers engaging in business-related activities, such as attending conferences, meetings, or exploring investment opportunities.
- The requirements for a business visa may include an invitation letter from a Nicaraguan company or institution and proof of financial means to support your stay.

Student Visa

Students planning to study in Nicaragua, whether for short courses or full academic programs, require a student visa.

The student visa usually requires a letter of acceptance from a Nicaraguan educational institution and proof of financial support.

Work Visa

Individuals intending to work in Nicaragua need a work visa, which is typically sponsored by a Nicaraguan employer.

- The employer must provide the necessary documentation, such as a work contract and company registration details, for the visa application.

Residency Visa

- The residency visa is for individuals planning to live in Nicaragua on a long-term basis.
- There are different categories of residency visas, including pensioner's residency, investor's residency, and family reunion residency, each with specific requirements.

Visa Exemptions for Nicaragua

Visa-Free Countries

- Citizens of several countries can enter Nicaragua without a visa for short stays. The duration of visa-free stays varies from 30 days to 90 days, depending on the country of citizenship.
- Some countries eligible for visa exemptions include the United States, Canada, the European Union member states, Australia, New Zealand, and many South American countries.

Central American Common Market (CACM) Citizens

- Citizens of countries within the Central American Common Market, which includes Guatemala, El Salvador, Honduras, and Costa Rica, can enter Nicaragua without a visa for an indefinite period.

Mercosur Member States

Citizens of Mercosur member states, such as Argentina, Brazil, and Uruguay, can enter Nicaragua visa-free for up to 90 days.

Taiwanese Passport Holders

Taiwanese passport holders can enter Nicaragua without a visa for stays of up to 90 days.

Essential Entry Requirements

Passport Validity

Ensure that your passport is valid for at least six months beyond your planned departure date from Nicaragua.

Proof of Sufficient Funds

Immigration authorities may require you to show proof of sufficient funds to cover your expenses during your stay in Nicaragua. This can be in the form of bank statements or an invitation letter from a sponsor if applicable.

Return or Onward Ticket

You may need to present a confirmed return or onward ticket to show that you have plans to leave Nicaragua at the end of your authorized stay.

Yellow Fever Vaccination Certificate

A yellow fever vaccination certificate is required if you are traveling from a country with a risk of yellow fever transmission. Check the list of affected countries to determine if you need this vaccination.

Visa Application Process

If your nationality requires a visa to enter Nicaragua or if you plan to stay for longer periods with a specific visa, follow these steps to apply:

Contact a Nicaraguan Consulate or Embassy

Locate the nearest Nicaraguan consulate or embassy in your country to inquire about the visa application process and requirements.

Gather the Required Documents

Collect all necessary documents for the specific visa type, such as passport copies, passport-sized photos, invitation letters, financial proof, and travel itinerary.

Complete the Visa Application Form

Obtain the official visa application form from the consulate or embassy and fill it out accurately and legibly.

Submit the Application

Submit the visa application and all supporting documents to the Nicaraguan consulate or embassy along with the appropriate visa fee. Apply well in advance of your chosen travel dates as processing times can vary.

Attend an Interview (if required)

Some visa categories may require an interview as part of the application process. Prepare for the interview by familiarizing

Nicaragua Travel Guide

yourself with the purpose of your trip and answering questions confidently.

Wait for Visa Approval

After submitting your application, await notification of visa approval. Once approved, you will receive the visa stamped in your passport.

Visa Extensions

If you find yourself in Nicaragua and wish to extend your stay beyond the permitted duration, it's essential to apply for a visa extension before your original visa expires. Contact the Nicaraguan immigration authorities or visit the immigration office in Managua to inquire about the extension process and requirements.

Overstaying

It's crucial to adhere to the visa regulations and not overstay your authorized period in Nicaragua. Overstaying can result in fines, deportation, or entry bans, affecting future travels to the country.

By following the guidelines for visa applications and preparing the necessary documentation, you'll be well-prepared to explore the wonders of Nicaragua, from its stunning landscapes to its vibrant cultural heritage. Remember to adhere to the visa regulations and entry requirements to ensure a trouble-free journey as you immerse yourself in the beauty and warmth of this captivating Central American destination.

Health and Vaccination Recommendations for Traveling to Nicaragua

Ensuring good health is crucial when traveling to any destination, and Nicaragua is no exception. Understanding the health risks and necessary vaccinations can help you prepare for a safe and enjoyable trip. In this comprehensive guide, we will explore health considerations, common health risks, and vaccination recommendations to help you stay healthy during your adventure in Nicaragua.

Health Considerations

Travel Health Consultation

Before traveling to Nicaragua, schedule a visit to a travel health specialist or a travel clinic. Discuss your travel plans, medical history, and any pre-existing conditions to receive personalized health recommendations for your trip.

Travel Insurance

Purchase comprehensive travel insurance that includes medical coverage and emergency medical evacuation. It's essential to have insurance that covers medical expenses, especially if you need to seek medical attention while in Nicaragua.

Medical Facilities

Major cities in Nicaragua, such as Managua, Granada, and Leon, have modern medical facilities and hospitals. However, medical resources may be limited in remote areas, so plan accordingly.

Prescription Medications

If you take prescription medications, ensure you have an ample supply for the duration of your trip. Carry medications in their original containers, and consider carrying a prescription or letter from your doctor explaining the need for the medication.

Food and Water Safety

To prevent foodborne illnesses, drink bottled or boiled water and avoid consuming raw or undercooked foods. Stick to well-cooked and freshly prepared meals from reputable establishments.

Mosquito-Borne Diseases

Nicaragua is a region where mosquito-borne diseases like dengue, Zika virus, and chikungunya are prevalent. To lower your risk of getting bitten by mosquitoes, wear long sleeves and pants and sleep with a mosquito net.

Altitude Sickness

If you plan to visit higher altitudes, such as in the northern highlands, be aware of altitude sickness symptoms and take necessary precautions, like acclimatizing slowly and staying hydrated.

Sun Protection

Nicaragua's tropical climate means intense sun exposure. Wear protective clothing, use sunscreen with a high SPF, and seek shade from the sun when it is at its peak.

Vaccination Recommendations

Routine Vaccinations

Ensure you are up-to-date on routine vaccinations, such as measles, mumps, rubella (MMR), diphtheria, tetanus, pertussis (DTaP), varicella (chickenpox), and the annual influenza vaccine.

Hepatitis A

The Hepatitis A vaccine is recommended for all travelers to Nicaragua, as the virus can be contracted through contaminated food and water.

Hepatitis B

The Hepatitis B vaccine is advisable for travelers engaging in activities that may involve contact with bodily fluids, such as medical procedures, tattooing, or sexual activities.

Typhoid

The Typhoid vaccine is recommended for travelers who may consume contaminated food or water, particularly in rural areas.

Yellow Fever

A yellow fever vaccination certificate is required if you are arriving from or transiting through a country with a risk of yellow fever transmission. Check the list of affected countries before traveling to Nicaragua.

Rabies

The Rabies vaccine is recommended for travelers who may have increased exposure to animals or plan to engage in activities like wildlife photography or animal handling.

Malaria

Nicaragua has reported some cases of malaria, particularly in rural areas. Consult with a travel health specialist to determine if antimalarial medication is necessary based on your travel itinerary and the time of year.

Preventing Mosquito-Borne Diseases

Zika Virus

Pregnant women or those planning to become pregnant should be aware of the risk of Zika virus transmission in Nicaragua. Consult with a healthcare professional for specific advice and take necessary precautions.

Dengue and Chikungunya

Protect yourself from mosquito bites by using insect repellent, wearing long sleeves and pants, and staying in accommodations with screened windows or air conditioning.

Food and Water Safety

Safe Drinking Water

Drink bottled or boiled water. Avoid consuming tap water, and use bottled water to brush your teeth.

Food Handling

Eat only well-cooked and freshly prepared foods from reputable establishments. Avoid street food and unpeeled fruits and vegetables.

Altitude Sickness

Gradual Acclimatization

If you plan to visit higher altitudes, take time to acclimatize gradually. Avoid intense physical activity during the first couple of days.

Sun Protection

Sunscreen and Protective Clothing

Use sunscreen with a high SPF, and wear wide-brimmed hats, sunglasses, and light-colored, loose-fitting clothing to protect yourself from the sun.

By taking these health precautions and staying informed, you'll be well-prepared to explore the natural beauty, cultural heritage, and vibrant landscapes of Nicaragua, creating cherished memories that will last a lifetime. Remember that good health practices not only ensure your well-being but also contribute to responsible and sustainable travel, leaving a positive impact on the communities and environments you encounter during your journey.

Packing Essentials for Your Trip to Nicaragua

Packing for your trip to Nicaragua requires thoughtful consideration of the diverse landscapes, climate, and cultural activities you'll encounter. From exploring colonial cities to hiking volcanoes and relaxing on pristine beaches, this comprehensive guide will help you pack efficiently and ensure you have all the essentials for a comfortable and memorable journey in this enchanting Central American destination.

Clothing

Lightweight Clothing

Nicaragua has a tropical climate, so pack lightweight and breathable clothing to stay comfortable in the heat. Cotton and moisture-wicking fabrics are ideal.

T-shirts and Tops

Pack a mix of short-sleeved and sleeveless tops for everyday wear. Opt for bright colors and patterns to blend in with the vibrant surroundings.

Long Sleeves and Pants

Bring a few long-sleeved shirts and lightweight pants for sun protection and to guard against mosquito bites, especially during evenings.

Swimwear

Don't forget to pack your swimwear, as Nicaragua boasts beautiful beaches and opportunities for water activities.

Rain Gear

If you're traveling during the rainy season, pack a lightweight rain jacket or poncho to stay dry during sudden downpours.

Comfortable Walking Shoes

Invest in comfortable walking shoes or sneakers for exploring cities, hiking, and walking on various terrains.

Sandals or Flip-Flops

Pack sandals or flip-flops for beach days and casual outings. They are also convenient for easily slipping on and off in humid climates.

Hat and Sunglasses

Bring a wide-brimmed hat and polarized sunglasses to protect yourself from the sun's rays.

Travel Accessories

Backpack or Daypack

A sturdy backpack or daypack is essential for day trips, hikes, and carrying your essentials while exploring.

Reusable Water Bottle

Stay hydrated by carrying a reusable water bottle. You can fill it up with filtered or bottled water as needed.

Travel Towel

Consider packing a quick-drying travel towel, especially if you plan to visit beaches or engage in water activities.

Travel Pillow and Eye Mask

For long journeys or flights, a travel pillow and eye mask can help you get some rest and arrive refreshed.

Mosquito Repellent

Pack mosquito repellent with DEET to protect yourself from mosquito bites, especially during evenings and in rural areas.

Sunscreen and Aloe Vera Gel

Protect your skin from the sun's rays with sunscreen, and pack aloe vera gel to soothe sunburns.

Portable Charger and Power Adapter

Keep your devices charged with a portable charger, and don't forget a power adapter to fit Nicaragua's electrical outlets (Type A and Type B).

Camera and Waterproof Cover

Capture the stunning landscapes and moments during your trip with a camera. Bring a waterproof cover to protect it from unexpected rain.

Documents and Essentials

Passport and Visa

Carry your passport with at least six months of validity beyond your planned departure date. Include any required visas or travel documents.

Travel Insurance Documents

Keep a copy of your travel insurance documents and emergency contact details handy.

Printed Itinerary and Hotel Reservations

Have a printed copy of your travel itinerary, hotel reservations, and important contact information in case of any internet or battery issues.

Money and Credit Cards

Bring sufficient cash in Nicaraguan Cordoba (NIO) or U.S. dollars, as well as credit/debit cards. To prevent any complications with overseas transactions, let your bank know about your vacation intentions.

Photocopies and Electronic Copies

Make photocopies and electronic copies of your important documents, such as your passport, travel insurance, and visa, to keep as backups.

First Aid Kit

Basic Medications

Pack a small first aid kit with essentials like pain relievers, antihistamines, antacids, motion sickness medication, and any prescription medications you may need.

Band-Aids and Adhesive Tape

Carry band-aids and adhesive tape for minor cuts and blisters.

Antibacterial Ointment

Include an antibiotic ointment to treat minor wounds.

Insect Bite Cream

Bring insect bite cream to relieve discomfort from mosquito bites.

Diarrhea Medication

Include anti-diarrheal medication in case of stomach upset.

Antiseptic Wipes

Carry antiseptic wipes for cleaning wounds or surfaces.

Personal Items

Toiletries

Bring your essential toiletries, including toothpaste, toothbrush, shampoo, conditioner, soap, and any other personal care items you need.

Prescription Glasses or Contacts

If you wear glasses or contacts, pack an extra pair and your prescription in case of loss or damage.

Travel Laundry Kit

A small travel laundry kit can help you wash clothes while on the go.

Travel Journal and Pen

Record your experiences and memories in a travel journal.

Miscellaneous Items

Ziplock Bags

Pack some ziplock bags to keep small items organized and to protect electronics from moisture.

Multi-tool or Swiss Army Knife

A multi-tool or Swiss Army knife can come in handy for various tasks during your trip.

Language Guide or Dictionary

Consider bringing a language guide or dictionary to help with basic communication in Spanish.

With these packing essentials in tow, you'll be ready to explore Nicaragua's diverse landscapes, immerse yourself in its vibrant culture, and create cherished memories that will last a lifetime.

3

Exploring the Regions of Nicaragua

Nicaragua's diverse landscapes, rich history, and vibrant culture beckon travelers to explore its various regions. From bustling cities to serene beaches, lush rainforests to majestic volcanoes, each region offers unique experiences that showcase the country's natural beauty and cultural heritage. In this comprehensive guide, we will delve into the captivating regions of Nicaragua and highlight the top attractions, starting with the capital city, Managua.

Managua (Discovering the Heart of Nicaragua)

As the capital and largest city of Nicaragua, Managua holds a central place in the country's political, cultural, and economic landscape. Nestled between Lake Managua and Lake Nicaragua, this city is a vibrant hub where history, modernity, and natural beauty intersect. From historical landmarks to urban attractions, Managua offers a multifaceted experience that provides insight into Nicaragua's dynamic identity.

Top Attractions in Managua

Plaza de la Revolución (Revolution Square)

Plaza de la Revolución stands as a symbol of Nicaragua's tumultuous history. It features the National Palace of Culture, the Old Cathedral of Managua, and a prominent statue of General Augusto Sandino, a national hero and leader of the resistance against U.S. intervention.

Loma de Tiscapa

Loma de Tiscapa is a historic hill that offers panoramic views of Managua and Lake Managua. At its peak, you'll find the silhouette of Augusto Sandino on a hilltop, offering both a symbol of the past and a captivating vista of the city.

Old Cathedral of Managua (Catedral de Santiago)

The Old Cathedral of Managua, also known as Catedral de Santiago, is a powerful reminder of the 1972 earthquake that devastated the city. The cathedral's ruins stand as a poignant monument to that tragic event, offering a glimpse into the city's history and resilience.

Rubén Darío National Theater

Named after Nicaragua's celebrated poet, the Rubén Darío National Theater is a cultural gem that hosts various performances, including theater, dance, music, and art exhibitions. The neoclassical architecture adds to the charm of this artistic haven.

Puerto Salvador Allende

This waterfront area along Lake Managua offers a blend of entertainment, dining, and relaxation. Stroll along the promenade, enjoy lakeside dining, or hop on a boat tour to explore the lake's beauty.

Malecón de Managua

The Malecón is a popular boardwalk along the shores of Lake Managua, offering a serene space for leisurely walks, bike rides, and enjoying the lake breeze. It's an ideal spot to witness stunning sunsets over the water.

National Palace of Culture

The National Palace of Culture is a historical and cultural landmark that houses museums, galleries, and exhibitions showcasing Nicaraguan art, history, and culture.

Salvador Allende Port

Named after Chile's former president, Salvador Allende Port is a recreational area with shops, restaurants, and even a small amusement park. It's a popular spot for families and offers a view of Lake Managua.

Los Robles District

Los Robles is a trendy neighborhood known for its upscale restaurants, cafes, boutiques, and art galleries. It's a great place to experience Managua's contemporary urban scene.

Montelimar Beach

While not within the city limits, Montelimar Beach is easily accessible from Managua and offers a relaxing coastal escape. Enjoy the sandy shores, calm waters, and beachfront resorts for a day of leisure.

Cultural Insights

Managua's attractions reflect its journey through history, from the devastating earthquake that reshaped the cityscape to the cultural resilience that has shaped its modern identity. The city's mix of contemporary architecture, historical landmarks, and vibrant cultural spaces offer a glimpse into Nicaragua's complex past and vibrant present.

Practical Tips

Transportation

Getting around Managua is possible by taxi, public transportation, or ridesharing apps. Taxis should be negotiated with the driver before starting the journey.

Language

Spanish is the official language, and while English is spoken in some tourist areas, having basic Spanish phrases will be helpful.

Safety

Exercise caution, especially in crowded areas, and avoid displaying valuable items or large amounts of cash.

Climate

Managua has a tropical climate with a rainy season from May to October and a dry season from November to April. Dress comfortably and carry an umbrella or raincoat during the rainy months.

Currency

The Nicaraguan Cordoba (NIO) is the official currency.

Time Zone

Nicaragua operates on Central Standard Time (CST), which is UTC-6.

Exploring Accommodation Options in Managua

As the capital and largest city of Nicaragua, Managua offers a wide range of accommodation options to suit different preferences and budgets. From luxurious hotels to budget-friendly hostels and charming boutique stays, the city caters to the needs of both leisure and business travelers. In this comprehensive guide, we will provide you with an extensive list of 30 accommodation options in Managua, ensuring you have a comfortable and convenient stay while exploring this vibrant Central American city.

Luxury Hotels

- InterContinental Managua at Metrocentro Mall: A five-star hotel located within the Metrocentro Mall complex, offering upscale amenities, spacious rooms, and easy access to shopping and entertainment.

- Real InterContinental Metrocentro Managua: A luxurious hotel with elegant rooms, a spa, an outdoor pool, and several dining options, all situated near the popular Metrocentro Mall.
- Hotel Crowne Plaza Managua: Featuring modern rooms, an outdoor pool, a fitness center, and various dining options, this hotel provides a comfortable stay for business and leisure travelers.
- Barceló Managua: A stylish hotel with contemporary rooms, a rooftop pool, a fitness center, and a convenient location near major attractions.
- Hotel Seminole: Known for its elegant colonial-style architecture, this hotel offers well-appointed rooms, a pool, and a tranquil garden atmosphere.

Mid-Range Hotels

- Hotel Camino Real Managua: Offering comfortable rooms, a pool, and easy access to major highways and the airport.
- Hotel Seminole Plaza: A sister property to Hotel Seminole, this hotel boasts comfortable rooms and a central location near restaurants and shopping.
- Hotel Los Robles: Situated in the upscale Los Robles neighborhood, this hotel offers cozy rooms, a garden, and proximity to dining and entertainment options.
- Hotel Mansion Teodolinda: Known for its warm hospitality, this hotel provides comfortable rooms, a pool, and a convenient location in the city.
- Holiday Inn Express Managua: Offering modern amenities, including free breakfast and Wi-Fi, this hotel is suitable for both business and leisure travelers.

Budget-Friendly Accommodations

- Hotel Hex Managua: A budget-friendly option with basic amenities, conveniently located near the Metrocentro Mall.
- Hotel Europeo: Providing simple and clean rooms, this hotel is centrally located and offers good value for budget-conscious travelers.
- Hotel Don Carmelo: A charming option with affordable rooms, situated in a quiet neighborhood and offering easy access to the city's attractions.
- Hotel Estrella: A family-run budget hotel with comfortable accommodations and a friendly atmosphere.
- Hotel Mozonte: A budget-friendly choice with clean rooms, a pool, and an on-site restaurant.

Boutique Stays

- La Pyramide: A boutique hotel with unique pyramid-shaped architecture, offering cozy rooms, a garden, and a relaxed ambiance.
- Hotel Contempo: Known for its modern design and artistic touches, this boutique hotel offers stylish rooms and a creative atmosphere.
- El Mirador Suites and Lounge: A boutique hotel with suites that provide a comfortable stay and panoramic views of the city.
- Hotel Los Pinos: Offering a blend of contemporary and traditional Nicaraguan design, this boutique hotel features comfortable rooms and a serene courtyard.
- Hotel La Posada de Manolo: A charming boutique hotel with rustic charm, located in a quiet residential area.

Apartment and Extended Stay Options

- Suites and Apartments Santo Domingo: Offering spacious suites and apartments with kitchenettes, suitable for extended stays.
- Apart Hotel Villa Angelo: Providing fully equipped apartments with kitchen facilities, making it ideal for those looking for a home-away-from-home experience.
- Apartamentos Los Angeles: Offering self-catering apartments with modern amenities, situated in a convenient location.
- Hotel Suites La María: A property with apartment-style accommodations, featuring a pool and a peaceful environment.
- Apart Hotel Nicaragua: Providing apartment-style living with kitchenettes, this hotel is great for travelers seeking a longer stay.

Hostels and Guesthouses

- Pachamama Hostel Managua: A social and laid-back hostel offering dormitory and private rooms, as well as a communal kitchen and garden.
- Hostal Monte Cristi: A cozy guesthouse with budget-friendly accommodations and a welcoming atmosphere.
- Hostal La Casa de los Abuelos: Known for its friendly staff and relaxed vibe, this guesthouse offers affordable rooms and a communal kitchen.
- Hostal Real Los Robles: A guesthouse with a homey atmosphere, offering simple rooms and a convenient location in the Los Robles neighborhood.
- Backpackers Inn: A budget-friendly hostel with dormitory-style accommodations and communal areas, perfect for backpackers and solo travelers.

As you explore the city's attractions, immerse yourself in its culture, and connect with its people, your chosen accommodation will serve as a welcoming base from which to embark on your Nicaraguan adventure.

Granada (A Colonial Gem on Lake Nicaragua)

Granada, often referred to as the "Jewel of Nicaragua," is one of the country's most picturesque and historically significant cities. Located on the northeastern shore of Lake Nicaragua, Granada exudes a sense of timeless elegance with its well-preserved colonial architecture, cobblestone streets, and vibrant culture. As one of the oldest cities in the Americas, Granada's history is intertwined with Spanish colonization, trade, and the struggles of independence, making it a treasure trove of stories and experiences for visitors.

Top Attractions in Granada

Parque Central (Central Park)

The heart of Granada, this bustling park is surrounded by colonial buildings, cafes, and vendors.

Cathedral of Granada

A stunning example of Spanish colonial architecture, the cathedral is an iconic landmark with a towering façade and intricate interior.

La Merced Church

Known for its vibrant yellow façade and stunning bell tower, La Merced is one of Granada's most recognizable churches.

Iglesia de Xalteva

This historic church is a testament to Granada's early history and features a distinct blend of Spanish and indigenous design.

San Francisco Convent

An exquisite complex housing a museum and the famous "La Polvora" tower with panoramic views of Granada.

Lake Nicaragua

The city's proximity to Lake Nicaragua offers opportunities for boat tours, kayaking, and enjoying serene sunsets over the water.

Islets of Granada

A collection of small islands in Lake Nicaragua, each with its unique charm and wildlife, making for a captivating boat tour.

Chocolate Museum

Delve into the world of cacao and chocolate-making, learning about the traditional process and sampling delicious treats.

Mansion de Chocolate

A luxurious boutique hotel and museum showcasing the history of chocolate in the region.

Fortaleza La Polvora

An 18th-century fortress that once protected Granada from pirates and invaders, now offering historical exhibits and stunning views.

Mi Museo

A unique museum showcasing the pre-Columbian and indigenous history of Nicaragua.

Granada Market

Explore the local market for souvenirs, handicrafts, fresh produce, and an authentic taste of Nicaraguan life.

Granada Cemetery

A peaceful and historically significant cemetery with ornate mausoleums and sculptures.

Granada Horse Carriage Tour

Take a horse-drawn carriage ride through the city's charming streets to enjoy a leisurely sightseeing experience.

Calle La Calzada

A lively street lined with restaurants, bars, shops, and vibrant street art, perfect for dining and socializing.

Los Poetas Park

A tranquil park dedicated to Nicaraguan poets, offering shaded spots for relaxation and contemplation.

Convento y Museo San Francisco

Explore the museum within the San Francisco Convent complex, showcasing religious art and historical artifacts.

ChocoMuseo Granada

A chocolate-themed museum where you can learn about cacao production, create your own chocolate, and sample unique flavors.

Guadalupe Church

A charming white church with a bell tower offering panoramic views of the city and surrounding landscapes.

Casa de los Leones

A historic mansion converted into a cultural center, hosting art exhibitions, workshops, and cultural events.

Unique Experiences in Granada

- Isletas de Granada Boat Tour: Embark on a boat tour of the Isletas, where you'll witness diverse bird species, quaint islands, and serene waters.
- Kayaking on Lake Nicaragua: Paddle your way through the calm waters of Lake Nicaragua, enjoying the scenic beauty and tranquility.
- Volcano Tours: Take a day trip to explore nearby volcanoes, such as Mombacho or Masaya, and experience their unique landscapes and natural wonders.
- Sunset Lake Cruises: Enjoy a relaxing cruise on Lake Nicaragua as the sun sets, painting the sky with a stunning array of colors.
- Spanish Language Classes: Immerse yourself in the local culture by taking Spanish language classes in Granada's language schools.

- Cooking Workshops: Learn to prepare traditional Nicaraguan dishes, such as gallo pinto and vigorón, in cooking workshops.
- Artisan Workshops: Engage in workshops where you can learn about local craftsmanship, from pottery to weaving.

Travel Tips for Exploring Granada

- Currency: The official currency is the Nicaraguan Cordoba (NIO) but in tourist destinations, US dollars are frequently accepted.
- Climate: Granada has a tropical climate with distinct wet and dry seasons. Bring comfortable clothing, insect repellant, and sunscreen.
- Safety: While Granada is generally safe, it's recommended to stay aware of your surroundings and exercise caution, especially at night.
- Transportation: Granada is a walkable city, but you can also use taxis or bicycle rentals to explore the area.
- Cultural Respect: Respect local customs and traditions, especially when visiting churches and religious sites.
- Local Cuisine: Try traditional Nicaraguan dishes like gallo pinto, vigorón, and nacatamal at local eateries.

Whether you're drawn to its colonial architecture, cultural treasures, or natural landscapes, Granada promises an enchanting journey that reveals the heart and soul of Nicaragua's historical and cultural heritage.

Exploring Accommodation Options in Granada

As you embark on a journey to discover the enchanting city of Granada, one of the most crucial decisions you'll make is where to

44

stay. Granada offers a diverse range of accommodations, each providing a unique blend of comfort, style, and immersion into the city's rich history and culture. From charming colonial-era boutique hotels to modern lodgings with stunning views, this comprehensive guide will help you navigate the options and find the perfect place to rest your head during your stay in Granada.

Boutique Hotels and Historic Inns

Granada's historic center is adorned with charming boutique hotels and inns that capture the essence of the city's colonial past. These accommodations often feature colonial architecture, courtyard gardens, and authentic décor, transporting you to a bygone era while providing modern comforts.

- Hotel Plaza Colon: Situated in Granada's main square, Hotel Plaza Colon offers elegant rooms with stunning views of Parque Central and the cathedral. The rooftop terrace provides a panoramic backdrop for enjoying breakfast or a sunset cocktail.
- Hotel Dario: Named after Nicaraguan poet Rubén Darío, this boutique hotel features exquisite Spanish colonial architecture, art-filled courtyards, and a relaxing pool area. Its central location makes it convenient for exploring Granada's attractions.
- Casa San Francisco: This restored colonial mansion offers luxurious suites and rooms, each uniquely designed to highlight Granada's rich history and culture. Enjoy peaceful courtyards, elegant dining, and personalized service.
- Hotel Xalteva: Located near Iglesia de Xalteva, this charming hotel offers a blend of modern amenities and colonial aesthetics. The rooftop terrace provides a

45

picturesque setting for relaxation and enjoying views of Granada's skyline.

Eco-Lodges and Nature Retreats

For those seeking a closer connection to nature, Granada offers eco-lodges and nature retreats that allow you to unwind in serene surroundings while contributing to sustainable tourism practices.

- Jicaro Island Ecolodge: Nestled on one of the islets of Granada, Jicaro Island Ecolodge offers private casitas with lake views, organic cuisine, and opportunities for kayaking, paddleboarding, and birdwatching.
- Mombacho Lodge: Located on the slopes of Volcano Mombacho, this eco-lodge offers rustic cabins immersed in cloud forest surroundings. Enjoy hiking trails, wildlife encounters, and panoramic vistas.

Modern Hotels and Resorts

Granada also boasts modern hotels and resorts that provide contemporary amenities, comfort, and convenience while still offering glimpses of the city's history and culture.

- Hotel Mansion de Chocolate: Combining luxury with history, this boutique hotel celebrates Granada's role in cacao production. Enjoy elegant rooms, a tranquil pool, and a museum dedicated to chocolate.
- Hotel Granada: A modern hotel with spacious rooms and suites, conveniently located near Granada's main attractions. The hotel's rooftop pool and bar offer a refreshing retreat after a day of exploration.

- Hotel La Polvora: Situated near Fortaleza La Polvora, this modern hotel offers comfortable accommodations, a relaxing courtyard, and proximity to both historical sites and the city center.

Guesthouses and Hostels

Budget-conscious travelers will find a range of guesthouses and hostels in Granada, offering affordable accommodations without sacrificing comfort or community.

- Hostel Oasis Granada: A laid-back hostel with colorful rooms, a pool, and a sociable atmosphere. It's an excellent option for backpackers and travelers looking to connect with fellow explorers.
- Casa Lucia: A cozy guesthouse with a communal kitchen, garden, and comfortable rooms. Enjoy a home-like atmosphere and the opportunity to interact with other guests.
- De Boca en Boca: This guesthouse provides a blend of affordability and authenticity, with rustic-style rooms and a central courtyard. It's a great option for travelers seeking a cozy and intimate stay.

Vacation Rentals

For a home-away-from-home experience, consider renting a vacation home or apartment in Granada. Vacation rentals allow you to have a private space and immerse yourself in the local neighborhood.

- Airbnb: Granada offers a wide range of Airbnb options, from colonial-style homes to modern apartments with local hosts who can provide insider tips.

47

- Vrbo: Explore vacation rental listings on Vrbo to find comfortable accommodations with amenities like kitchens and living areas.

Tips for Choosing Accommodations in Granada

- Location: Consider staying near Parque Central for easy access to Granada's main attractions, restaurants, and entertainment.
- Amenities: Determine which amenities are important to you, such as Wi-Fi, swimming pools, on-site restaurants, and airport transfers.
- Reviews and Ratings: Read reviews from previous guests to get insights into the quality of service, cleanliness, and overall experience.
- Local Character: Choose accommodations that capture Granada's unique charm, whether it's a colonial-style inn, an eco-lodge, or a modern boutique hotel.
- Budget: Granada offers a range of accommodations to suit different budgets. Plan your budget in advance and explore options that align with your preferences.

Whichever option you choose, you'll find yourself immersed in the city's rich history, culture, and natural beauty, creating a home base from which you can explore the enchanting streets, architectural wonders, and captivating landscapes that define Granada's allure.

Best Eateries in Granada

No journey is complete without indulging in the local culinary scene, and Granada offers a feast for the senses that captures the essence of Nicaraguan flavors and traditions. From bustling markets to charming cafes and elegant restaurants, Granada's eateries showcase a diverse range of dishes that reflect the country's cultural heritage and culinary creativity. In this comprehensive guide, we will delve into the best eateries that Granada has to offer, providing a mouthwatering tour of its dining landscape.

El Zaguan

Known for its elegant ambiance and exquisite menu, El Zaguan is a culinary gem in Granada. The restaurant is housed in a beautifully restored colonial mansion, offering both indoor and courtyard seating. The menu features a fusion of Nicaraguan and international flavors, with dishes like grilled meats, fresh seafood, and artisanal cocktails. Don't miss their decadent desserts, such as the coconut flan or chocolate lava cake.

The Garden Café

A beloved establishment nestled in the heart of Granada, The Garden Café delights visitors with its charming courtyard setting and delectable offerings. The menu showcases a blend of international and Nicaraguan dishes made from locally sourced ingredients. Enjoy dishes like mango ceviche, grilled chicken with chimichurri, and the signature "Bavarian Breakfast" featuring sausages, eggs, and fresh bread.

La Calzada Delicatessen

This cozy eatery on Calle La Calzada offers a variety of culinary delights, from hearty breakfast options to flavorful sandwiches, salads, and gourmet coffee. The restaurant's warm atmosphere and friendly staff create a welcoming environment for both locals and tourists. Try their famous chicken sandwich or the "Nicaraguan Breakfast" featuring gallo pinto and plantains.

La Gran Francia

Located within the historic Hotel La Gran Francia, this restaurant offers a refined dining experience with colonial charm. The menu showcases a blend of French and Nicaraguan cuisine, featuring dishes like grilled octopus, filet mignon, and seafood paella. The elegant courtyard setting adds to the overall ambiance, making it an ideal spot for a romantic dinner or special occasion.

Café de los Sueños

As the name suggests, Café de los Sueños (Café of Dreams) is a dreamy spot for coffee lovers and food enthusiasts alike. This café boasts a lush garden setting with colorful artwork and a relaxed atmosphere. Enjoy freshly brewed coffee, breakfast options, sandwiches, and an array of baked goods. The café's commitment to sustainability and community engagement is evident in its practices and offerings.

El Garaje

For those craving authentic Nicaraguan cuisine, El Garaje is a must-visit eatery. This unassuming restaurant offers a wide range of traditional dishes, from nacatamales and vigorón to carne asada and grilled fish. The casual setting and affordable prices make it a favorite among both locals and tourists seeking an authentic taste of Nicaraguan flavors.

Pan de Vida

A delightful bakery and café, Pan de Vida is known for its freshly baked bread, pastries, and artisanal treats. Whether you're looking for a morning coffee and pastry or a light lunch with sandwiches and salads, this charming spot offers a cozy and inviting environment to enjoy your meal.

Asados Juanita

If you're in the mood for a mouthwatering barbecue, Asados Juanita is the place to be. This rustic eatery specializes in grilled meats, sausages, and ribs cooked to perfection. The laid-back atmosphere and outdoor seating create a casual dining experience where you can relish the smoky flavors and hearty portions.

Street Food and Markets

Granada's local markets and street food vendors offer an authentic taste of Nicaraguan street cuisine. Visit the bustling Central Market for a variety of options, including grilled meats, fried plantains, yucca, and local snacks. Don't miss out on enjoying a traditional "fritanga" platter, featuring a mix of grilled meats and sides.

Cocina de Doña Haydée

For an immersive experience in Nicaraguan home cooking, Cocina de Doña Haydée provides a welcoming environment where you can savor traditional dishes made with love. The family-run restaurant offers a menu that changes daily, featuring staples like gallo pinto, tortillas, and flavorful stews.

Gardenia

Gardenia is a favorite among both locals and visitors, offering a menu that celebrates Nicaraguan ingredients and flavors. The restaurant's commitment to sustainability and local sourcing is evident in its dishes, which range from fresh seafood to vegetarian options. The vibrant atmosphere and garden setting create a memorable dining experience.

El Mediterráneo

If you're craving Mediterranean flavors, El Mediterráneo offers a refreshing departure from Nicaraguan cuisine. This restaurant presents a variety of dishes inspired by Mediterranean countries, such as Greece and Spain. Enjoy dishes like falafel, hummus, grilled seafood, and tapas in a relaxed and inviting setting.

Tips for Dining in Granada

- Try Local Specialties: Don't miss out on experiencing traditional Nicaraguan dishes like gallo pinto, vigorón, and nacatamales.
- Fresh Seafood: Being located near Lake Nicaragua, Granada offers an abundance of fresh seafood options that are worth trying.
- Street Food Adventure: Embrace the local street food scene for an authentic and affordable dining experience.
- Local Ingredients: Look for eateries that emphasize the use of locally sourced ingredients to support sustainable practices and savor the freshest flavors.
- Cultural Etiquette: Observe local customs and manners while dining, such as saying "buen provecho" (enjoy your meal) before starting to eat.

- Reservations: For popular restaurants, consider making reservations, especially during peak dining hours.

León (A Historical Gem)

León, often referred to as "León de los Caballeros," is a city that exudes a sense of grandeur and historical importance. Located in northwestern Nicaragua, León boasts a rich colonial past and a rebellious spirit that played a pivotal role in the nation's fight for independence and social justice. With its impressive architecture, cultural sites, and revolutionary history, León stands as a testament to Nicaragua's enduring spirit and the resilience of its people.

Historical Sites in León

León Cathedral (Catedral de León)

One of the most iconic landmarks in León, the León Cathedral is a UNESCO World Heritage Site and a masterpiece of colonial architecture. Built between 1747 and 1814, the cathedral features an exquisite baroque façade adorned with intricate carvings and statues. Its interior is equally captivating, with ornate altars, impressive frescoes, and a stunning collection of religious art. The cathedral's rooftop offers panoramic views of the city and surrounding landscapes, providing a unique perspective of León's historical and urban landscapes.

León Viejo

Situated near Lake Xolotlán, León Viejo is an archaeological site that offers a glimpse into the city's earliest colonial history. Founded in 1524, it was one of the first Spanish settlements in the Americas. The ruins of León Viejo showcase remnants of colonial buildings, streets, and fortifications, giving visitors a chance to explore the city's origins and learn about its historical significance.

Ortiz-Gurdian Foundation Art Center (Centro de Arte Fundación Ortiz-Gurdián)

Housed in a beautifully restored colonial mansion, this art center features an impressive collection of Nicaraguan and Latin American art. The exhibits span from pre-Columbian artifacts to contemporary works, offering insights into the region's artistic heritage and evolution.

Rubén Darío Museum (Museo Rubén Darío)

Named after Nicaragua's most celebrated poet, the Rubén Darío Museum is dedicated to the life and works of this literary figure. The museum showcases Darío's personal belongings, manuscripts, and memorabilia, providing visitors with a deeper understanding of his contributions to literature and culture.

Revolution Square (Plaza de la Revolución)

An emblematic site that carries the weight of Nicaragua's revolutionary history, Revolution Square features a towering monument of Sandino, the national hero who led the resistance against foreign intervention. The square serves as a gathering place for events, demonstrations, and commemorations, reflecting the city's commitment to social change and political activism.

León Art Gallery (Galería de Arte León)

This gallery showcases a diverse collection of contemporary art from Nicaraguan and international artists. With rotating exhibitions that cover various artistic mediums, the gallery provides insight into the modern artistic scene in León and beyond.

El Calvario Church (Iglesia El Calvario)

A colonial-era church known for its distinctive architecture and role in León's history. The church's rooftop offers panoramic views of the city, making it a popular spot for visitors seeking both spiritual and visual enrichment.

Museum of Traditions and Legends (Museo de Tradiciones y Leyendas)

Immerse yourself in Nicaragua's folklore and cultural heritage at this museum, where exhibits highlight traditional stories, myths, and customs of the region. The museum's displays provide a deeper appreciation for the cultural diversity that defines León and Nicaragua as a whole.

Juan José Quezada Espinoza Cultural Center

This cultural center celebrates the legacy of Juan José Quezada Espinoza, a prominent Nicaraguan intellectual and advocate for social justice. The center hosts cultural events, workshops, and exhibitions that promote education, culture, and social awareness.

Heroes and Martyrs Mausoleum (Maosoleo de los Héroes y Mártires)

Dedicated to the memory of those who lost their lives during the Sandinista Revolution, this mausoleum commemorates the sacrifices made by people who fought for social justice and equal rights. The site serves as a symbol of Nicaragua's resilience and the ongoing pursuit of a just society.

El Laborio Church (Iglesia El Laborio)

Another example of León's colonial architecture, El Laborio Church is known for its elegant façade and intricate details. The church's interior features ornate altars and religious artwork, providing a glimpse into the city's historical and spiritual heritage.

Recolección Church (Iglesia de la Recolección)

An architectural gem that reflects the influence of Spanish colonial architecture in León. The church's intricate façade and bell towers contribute to its aesthetic appeal, making it a favorite among visitors interested in historical and cultural exploration.

Tips for Exploring Historical Sites in León

- Guided Tours: Consider joining guided tours of historical sites to gain deeper insights into their significance and historical context.
- Opening Hours: Check the opening hours of historical sites in advance, as they may vary. Some sites may have specific visiting hours or days.
- Respectful Attire: When visiting religious sites, dress modestly out of respect for the cultural and spiritual significance of the places.
- Photography: Confirm whether photography is allowed within historical sites, as some locations may have restrictions.
- Local Guides: Engage with local guides or audio guides available at certain sites to enhance your understanding of their history.

- Cultural Awareness: Embrace the opportunity to learn about the local culture, history, and contributions that shaped León's identity.

As you explore these landmarks, you'll not only deepen your understanding of Nicaragua's history but also forge a connection with the stories, people, and movements that have shaped León's identity. Whether you're an enthusiast of architecture, art, or social change, León's historical sites provide a profound journey through time and a celebration of the human spirit's capacity to create, endure, and inspire.

Accommodation Choices in León: Creating Your Haven

Nestled amidst the historical treasures and vibrant culture of León, the choices for accommodation in this Nicaraguan city are as diverse as its history. Whether you seek the elegance of colonial-era mansions, the coziness of budget-friendly hostels, or the convenience of modern hotels, León offers a range of options to suit every traveler's preferences. In this comprehensive guide, we'll take a closer look at the accommodation choices available in León, providing insights into the unique features and experiences they offer.

Boutique Colonial Hotels

León's colonial architecture and historical significance are reflected in its boutique colonial hotels. These accommodations provide an immersive experience that transports you back in time while offering modern comforts.

- Hotel El Convento: Housed in a former convent, this boutique hotel offers elegant rooms with colonial-style furnishings. The central courtyard and pool area provide a tranquil setting for relaxation. The hotel's location near León Cathedral and other attractions adds to its appeal.
- Hotel La Perla: This charming hotel features well-appointed rooms with a blend of colonial and modern aesthetics. The rooftop terrace offers panoramic views of León's skyline and the nearby cathedral. With its central location and personalized service, Hotel La Perla is a popular choice among travelers.
- Hotel Azul: A boutique hotel that combines colonial architecture with contemporary design. The hotel's courtyard garden, elegant rooms, and artful décor create a welcoming and stylish ambiance.

Hostels and Guesthouses

For budget-conscious travelers or those seeking a social atmosphere, León offers a variety of hostels and guesthouses that provide comfortable accommodations and opportunities to connect with fellow travelers.

- Bigfoot Hostel: A vibrant and sociable hostel that offers dormitory-style accommodations, private rooms, and a range of activities for guests. With its pool area, bar, and lively atmosphere, Bigfoot Hostel is a hub for backpackers and adventure seekers.
- Lazybones Hostel: Known for its relaxed and friendly vibe, Lazybones Hostel offers dormitory beds and private rooms. The common areas, hammocks, and garden provide spaces for relaxation and mingling with fellow guests.

- Sonati Hostel: This eco-friendly hostel focuses on sustainability and community engagement. With its garden, rooftop terrace, and cultural events, Sonati Hostel offers a cozy and environmentally conscious lodging option.

Luxury Hotels and Resorts

For travelers seeking refined experiences and upscale amenities, León's luxury hotels and resorts provide elegance, comfort, and attentive service.

- Hotel Real Intercontinental Metrocentro: A modern luxury hotel located near León's main attractions. The hotel boasts spacious rooms, a spa, fitness facilities, and multiple dining options.
- Hacienda Puerta del Cielo Eco Lodge & Spa: Nestled in the countryside near León, this eco-lodge offers a secluded retreat surrounded by nature. Enjoy luxury accommodations, a spa, yoga classes, and breathtaking views.
- Hotel Mariposa: A boutique hotel that combines luxury with a central location. With its elegant rooms, pool, and personalized service, Hotel Mariposa offers a tranquil oasis in the heart of León.

Eco-Friendly Lodges and Retreats

For travelers seeking a deeper connection to nature and sustainable practices, León offers eco-friendly lodges and retreats that harmonize with the environment.

- Villas de Palermo Hotel and Resort: Located a short distance from León, this resort offers private villas with stunning views of the Pacific Ocean. Enjoy a range of amenities, including a pool, restaurant, and spa.

- La Flor de Sutiaba Ecolodge: Set in a natural reserve, this eco-lodge provides a rustic yet comfortable experience. With its emphasis on sustainability, La Flor de Sutiaba Ecolodge offers a serene escape from the bustling city.
- Rancho Esperanza: This eco-friendly lodge combines comfortable accommodations with a focus on sustainable practices. Set in a peaceful environment, Rancho Esperanza offers opportunities for relaxation and outdoor activities.

Vacation Rentals

For travelers who value privacy and independence, vacation rentals in León offer a home-away-from-home experience.

- Airbnb: Explore a range of vacation rental options on Airbnb, from apartments in the heart of the city to cozy casitas in quieter neighborhoods.
- Vrbo: Find vacation rentals on Vrbo that provide ample space, amenities like kitchens and living areas, and the opportunity to live like a local in León.

Cultural Homestays

For an immersive cultural experience, consider staying with local families who offer accommodations in their homes.

- Casa El Ojoche: This homestay provides guests with the chance to experience Nicaraguan family life and hospitality. Guests can participate in cooking classes, learn about local traditions, and engage with the community.

- Estrella Negra Homestay: Located just outside of León, this homestay offers a serene environment and opportunities to learn about sustainable living practices from the hosts.

Tips for Choosing Accommodations in León

- Location: Consider staying in accommodations that are centrally located or in neighborhoods that align with your preferences.
- Amenities: Determine which amenities are essential for your stay, such as Wi-Fi, breakfast, pool access, or on-site dining options.
- Reviews and Ratings: Read reviews from previous guests to gain insights into the quality of service, cleanliness, and overall experience.
- Cultural Respect: Respect local customs and traditions when staying in accommodations that offer cultural experiences.
- Budget: León offers a range of accommodations to suit different budgets. Plan your budget in advance and explore options that align with your preferences.
- Conclusion:

By selecting accommodations that align with your travel style and preferences, you'll create a haven that enhances your exploration of León's historical sites, local culture, and vibrant atmosphere. As you embark on this journey, you'll not only discover the city's treasures but also find a home where cherished memories are made.

Food and Drink Recommendations in León

León, a city rich in history and culture, extends its charm to the realm of gastronomy. From traditional Nicaraguan dishes that showcase the nation's culinary heritage to international flavors that reflect León's cosmopolitan spirit, the city offers a diverse array of food and drink options that cater to every palate. In this comprehensive guide, we'll delve into the food and drink recommendations that define León's culinary landscape, inviting you to savor the flavors and immerse yourself in the city's vibrant food scene.

Nacatamal

A quintessential Nicaraguan dish, the nacatamal is a hearty treat that combines flavors and textures in a flavorful package. This traditional dish consists of seasoned pork or chicken, rice, vegetables, and seasonings wrapped in maize dough and banana leaves, then steamed to perfection. The result is a mouthwatering blend of savory ingredients that encapsulate the essence of Nicaraguan comfort food. Locals often enjoy nacatamal for breakfast or as a satisfying midday meal.

Gallo Pinto

A staple of Nicaraguan cuisine, Gallo Pinto is a savory mixture of rice and black beans seasoned with onions, peppers, and spices. Often served alongside scrambled or fried eggs, this dish is a breakfast favorite that provides a hearty and flavorful start to the day.

Quesillo

Quesillo, also known as "Nicaraguan cheese tortilla," is a beloved street food that tantalizes the taste buds. It features a freshly made tortilla filled with soft white cheese, pickled onions, and a touch of sour cream. The combination of textures and flavors creates a delightful snack that locals and visitors alike relish.

Indio Viejo

Indio Viejo is a hearty stew that pays homage to Nicaragua's indigenous heritage. Made from shredded meat (usually beef or chicken), vegetables, and corn masa, the dish is seasoned with achiote and spices. The result is a flavorful and nourishing dish that exemplifies the fusion of indigenous and colonial influences in Nicaraguan cuisine.

Vigorón

A dish that embodies both tradition and taste, vigorón consists of yucca (cassava) topped with chicharrones (crispy pork belly) and a cabbage salad. The contrast of textures and flavors creates a delightful balance that captures the essence of Nicaraguan street food.

Fresh Seafood

Being situated near the Pacific Ocean, León offers an array of fresh seafood options that reflect its coastal location. Whether you're savoring grilled fish, shrimp ceviche, or seafood platters, you'll enjoy flavors that are emblematic of Nicaragua's maritime culture.

Rondón

This flavorful seafood soup is a Caribbean-inspired dish that showcases the diverse influences on Nicaraguan cuisine. Combining coconut milk, seafood, yucca, and plantains, rondón delivers a rich and aromatic taste that transports you to the coastal regions of the country.

Craft Beer

León has embraced the craft beer movement, and you'll find a variety of local breweries offering innovative brews that cater to different preferences. Whether you're a fan of hoppy IPAs, smooth stouts, or refreshing lagers, exploring León's craft beer scene is a must for beer enthusiasts.

Cacao-Themed Treats

León's historical connection to cacao production is celebrated through various cacao-themed treats. From chocolate bars and truffles to hot chocolate infused with local spices, indulging in cacao-based delights is a sensory experience that pays homage to Nicaragua's past and present.

Café de Olla

Nicaraguan coffee culture is alive and well in León, where you can savor a cup of Café de Olla. This traditional coffee is brewed with spices like cinnamon and cloves, creating a warm and aromatic beverage that captures the essence of Nicaraguan flavors.

Raspados

Beat the heat with a refreshing raspado, a shaved ice treat that comes in a variety of flavors, often topped with condensed milk. Whether you opt for tropical fruit flavors or classic favorites, raspados offer a delightful way to cool down and satisfy your sweet tooth.

Local Markets

Exploring León's local markets, such as Mercado Central, offers a chance to sample an array of authentic Nicaraguan street food and snacks. From fried plantains to tamales, these markets provide a sensory journey through the city's culinary traditions.

International Flavors

León's cosmopolitan atmosphere is reflected in its international dining options. From Italian pasta and pizza to Middle Eastern falafel and Mediterranean dishes, the city's diverse palate ensures that you can enjoy global flavors without leaving its vibrant streets.

Tips for Enjoying Food and Drink in León

- Local Guidance: Seek recommendations from locals for the best places to enjoy traditional dishes and local specialties.
- Street Food: Embrace the local street food scene for an authentic culinary experience. Look for vendors with a steady stream of customers, a sign of delicious offerings.
- Dining Hours: Nicaraguan dining customs often include a leisurely pace. Lunch is typically the main meal of the day, and dinner is enjoyed later in the evening.

- Cultural Etiquette: Observe local customs and manners when dining, such as saying "buen provecho" (enjoy your meal) before starting to eat.
- Fresh and Seasonal: Savor the flavors of León's cuisine by opting for dishes made with fresh, local, and seasonal ingredients.
- Try Something New: While enjoying traditional Nicaraguan dishes is a must, don't hesitate to explore international options for a culinary adventure.

As you savor the flavors, engage with local vendors, and discover the city's gastronomic treasures, you'll not only satisfy your appetite but also forge a connection with the cultural richness that defines León's identity.

San Juan del Sur: A Coastal Haven

San Juan del Sur, located in the southern part of Nicaragua, boasts a breathtaking coastline, making it a prime destination for beach lovers, surf enthusiasts, and travelers seeking a laid-back yet invigorating escape. With its vibrant energy and stunning landscapes, San Juan del Sur has evolved from a fishing village to a lively hub that caters to diverse interests and preferences. Whether you're lounging on the sand, riding the waves, enjoying local cuisine, or dancing the night away, San Juan del Sur promises a dynamic experience that resonates with both tranquility and adventure.

Beaches and Activities in San Juan del Sur

Playa San Juan del Sur

The namesake beach of the town, Playa San Juan del Sur, welcomes visitors with its crescent-shaped shoreline, golden sands, and picturesque views. The beach is an ideal spot for sunbathing, swimming, and relaxing under the sun. As the main beach in town, it offers a range of amenities, including beachfront bars, restaurants, and water sports rentals.

Playa Maderas

A haven for surfers, Playa Maderas is known for its consistent waves and vibrant surf culture. Whether you're a seasoned surfer or a beginner, you'll find opportunities to catch the perfect wave. The beach's relaxed atmosphere and breathtaking sunsets also make it a popular spot for beachgoers and photographers.

Playa Hermosa

True to its name, Playa Hermosa enchants visitors with its beauty and tranquility. This pristine beach is surrounded by lush vegetation, creating a serene backdrop for relaxation. While swimming may be limited due to strong currents, the beach offers a quiet escape for sunbathing, picnicking, and immersing yourself in nature.

Playa Remanso

With its calm waters and gentle waves, Playa Remanso is a family-friendly beach that's perfect for swimming and novice surfers. The beach's laid-back atmosphere and shaded areas make it an inviting spot for spending the day.

Playa Yankee

For those seeking seclusion and a more remote beach experience, Playa Yankee offers a rugged shoreline and pristine surroundings. While the beach's strong currents make swimming less common, it's a popular spot for experienced surfers and beachcombers looking to escape the crowds.

Water Sports and Activities

Beyond beach lounging, San Juan del Sur offers a range of water-based activities, including surfing, stand-up paddleboarding, kayaking, and fishing. Surf schools and rental shops cater to beginners and experienced surfers alike, allowing you to ride the waves under expert guidance.

Hiking and Nature Exploration

Embark on hikes to nearby viewpoints, such as the Christ of the Mercy statue, for panoramic views of the town and coastline. Guided tours to local forests and reserves offer opportunities to spot wildlife and immerse yourself in Nicaragua's natural beauty.

Accommodation Selection in San Juan del Sur

Boutique Beachfront Hotels

Experience the allure of San Juan del Sur's coastline by staying in boutique beachfront hotels that offer direct access to the sea and stunning ocean views.

- Morgan's Rock Hacienda & Ecolodge: Nestled within a private reserve, this eco-lodge offers luxurious bungalows with ocean views. Its commitment to sustainability and nature conservation adds to the allure of its beachfront setting.

- Pelican Eyes Resort & Spa: Perched on a hillside, this resort provides breathtaking views of San Juan del Sur's bay. With its infinity pools, lush gardens, and luxurious accommodations, Pelican Eyes offers a tranquil escape with easy access to the town's attractions.
- Aqua Wellness Resort: This eco-friendly resort is situated within a lush tropical setting and offers treehouse-style accommodations. With its private beach, yoga pavilion, and wellness-focused amenities, Aqua Wellness Resort provides a rejuvenating experience.

Hostels and Surf Lodges

For budget-conscious travelers and surf enthusiasts seeking a social atmosphere, San Juan del Sur's hostels and surf lodges offer comfortable accommodations and opportunities to connect with fellow travelers.

- Casa Oro: Known for its vibrant social scene, Casa Oro offers both private rooms and dormitory-style accommodations. The hostel's communal spaces, pool, and events make it a hub for backpackers.
- Hulakai Hotel: Combining comfortable accommodations with a surf-friendly atmosphere, Hulakai Hotel caters to travelers seeking an affordable and convenient base for surf adventures.

Vacation Rentals and Guesthouses

For those seeking privacy and flexibility, vacation rentals and guesthouses provide a home-away-from-home experience with a touch of local charm.

- Airbnb: Explore a variety of vacation rental options on Airbnb, from cozy guesthouses to beachfront condos that offer personalized space and amenities.
- Vrbo: Discover vacation rentals on Vrbo that provide the comforts of home while allowing you to immerse yourself in San Juan del Sur's coastal lifestyle.

Eco-Friendly Retreats

Embrace sustainable living and connect with nature by choosing eco-friendly retreats that prioritize environmental consciousness.

- El Coco Loco Resort: Known for its eco-friendly practices and commitment to the local community, El Coco Loco Resort offers unique accommodations in rustic-chic cabins and beachfront casitas.
- TreeCasa Resort: Set in a lush jungle environment, TreeCasa Resort combines eco-conscious accommodations with wellness experiences, yoga classes, and opportunities for relaxation.

Dining and Nightlife in San Juan del Sur

Local Seafood and Cuisine

San Juan del Sur's dining scene celebrates fresh seafood and traditional Nicaraguan flavors, offering a culinary journey that reflects the city's coastal location.

- El Timón: This beachfront restaurant specializes in seafood dishes that highlight the day's catch. Enjoy ocean views while savoring ceviche, grilled fish, and other seafood delights.

- The Black Whale: Known for its seafood and international cuisine, The Black Whale offers a diverse menu that caters to different tastes. With its oceanfront location, it's a popular spot for sunset dining.
- Comedor La Piscina: A local gem that offers a variety of Nicaraguan dishes, including seafood, soups, and traditional platters. The restaurant's casual atmosphere and local flavors make it a favorite among residents.

International Flavors

San Juan del Sur's dining options extend beyond traditional cuisine, offering international flavors that cater to diverse palates.

- Simon Says: This restaurant features a menu with global influences, offering everything from burgers and sandwiches to Mediterranean-inspired dishes. Live music and a lively atmosphere contribute to its appeal.
- Barrio Café: A popular choice for those craving Mexican cuisine, Barrio Café offers tacos, burritos, and other flavorful dishes. Its vibrant setting and tequila selection create a festive ambiance.

Beachfront Dining

Immerse yourself in the coastal experience by dining at beachfront establishments that offer stunning ocean views and a relaxed ambiance.

- El Camino Del Sol: This beachfront restaurant serves a variety of dishes that highlight fresh seafood and local ingredients. With its location on Playa Maderas, it's an excellent spot for post-surf dining.

71

- Coco Beach Restaurant & Bar: Located on Playa Hermosa, this beachfront restaurant offers a menu that emphasizes seafood and tropical flavors. Enjoy meals with your toes in the sand and panoramic ocean views.

Nightlife and Socializing

When the sun sets, San Juan del Sur's nightlife comes alive with a mix of beachside bars, lively clubs, and social gatherings.

- PachaMama: A well-known beachfront bar that hosts parties, live music, and themed events. PachaMama's open-air setting and fire shows contribute to its vibrant atmosphere.
- The Loose Moose: A favorite among travelers, The Loose Moose is a lively bar that offers a mix of music genres, dance floors, and a laid-back vibe. Enjoy signature cocktails and socialize with fellow visitors.

Evening Beach Gatherings

One of the unique charms of San Juan del Sur is the tradition of nightly beach gatherings, where travelers and locals come together to enjoy bonfires, music, and the beauty of the ocean under the moonlight.

Tips for Enjoying San Juan del Sur's Offerings

- Sun Protection: Whether you're lounging on the beach or exploring the town, don't forget sunscreen, hats, and protective clothing to shield yourself from the sun.
- Water Activities: Follow safety guidelines and instructions when participating in water sports and activities to ensure a safe and enjoyable experience.

72

- Local Recommendations: Seek recommendations from locals for the best beaches, dining spots, and nightlife experiences. Locals often know the hidden gems and off-the-beaten-path venues.
- Cultural Etiquette: When dining and socializing, respect local customs and manners to ensure a positive and respectful interaction with residents and fellow travelers.

As you navigate the waves, savor the flavors, and embrace the energy of this coastal haven, you'll uncover the rich tapestry of experiences that make San Juan del Sur a destination that lingers in your memory as a true paradise.

4

Immersing in Culture of Nicaragua (Embracing Traditions and Customs)

Nicaragua's rich cultural tapestry weaves together indigenous heritage, colonial influences, and modern dynamics, creating a diverse and vibrant mosaic that beckons travelers to delve into its authenticity. From local traditions that reflect deep-rooted beliefs to customs that highlight hospitality and communal bonds, immersing in Nicaragua's culture is a journey of discovery and connection. In this comprehensive guide, we'll explore the local traditions and customs that define Nicaragua's cultural identity, offering insights into the heart of the nation's soul.

Local Traditions and Customs

Semana Santa (Holy Week)

A cornerstone of Nicaraguan religious and cultural life, Semana Santa is celebrated with profound devotion and elaborate processions in various towns and cities. During Holy Week, communities commemorate the Passion, Death, and Resurrection of Jesus Christ through parades, reenactments, and religious rituals. Streets are adorned with intricate sawdust carpets, and participants dress in biblical attire to honor the events of Easter.

Fiestas Patronales

These patron saint festivals celebrate the connection between faith and community. Each town has a patron saint, and their feast day is marked with lively celebrations that include processions, music, dancing, and traditional food. The festivities showcase Nicaragua's vibrant spirit and provide a glimpse into the intersection of religion and culture.

La Purísima

A November tradition, La Purísima celebrates the Immaculate Conception of the Virgin Mary. Families and neighbors create colorful altars adorned with flowers, candles, and religious images. Visitors are invited to go "a la Griteria," visiting different altars to sing hymns and receive treats, creating a harmonious blend of spirituality and social connection.

Gritería Chiquita

Taking place on December 7th, this mini-celebration is an extension of La Purísima. Children go door-to-door singing hymns and receiving small gifts and sweets from neighbors. The tradition fosters camaraderie and the sharing of blessings.

Día de la Independencia

On September 15th, Nicaragua commemorates its independence from Spanish rule with parades, dances, and patriotic displays. The festivities honor the nation's history and resilience, emphasizing unity and pride.

El Güegüense

This folkloric theatrical performance is a cultural masterpiece that dates back to the colonial era. El Güegüense is a satirical drama that combines indigenous, Spanish, and African influences, touching on social, political, and cultural themes. The performance highlights the enduring significance of traditional arts in conveying societal commentary.

Dance and Music

Music and dance are integral to Nicaragua's cultural fabric. Traditional dances like the "Palo de Mayo" showcase African and indigenous influences, while the "Gigantona" and "Enano Cabezón" are characters featured in processions and festivals, symbolizing colonial times. Marimba music, played on wooden xylophones, resonates with indigenous and mestizo heritage, while modern genres like reggaeton and hip-hop reflect contemporary cultural expressions.

Artisan Crafts

Nicaragua's artisan crafts embody centuries-old techniques and cultural motifs. Handwoven textiles, pottery, woodcarvings, and jewelry showcase indigenous creativity and artistic heritage. Visiting local markets and workshops offers a chance to appreciate the craftsmanship and stories behind each piece.

Hospitality and Friendliness

Nicaraguan culture is characterized by warmth and hospitality. Greetings are often accompanied by a handshake, hug, or kiss on the cheek, and people take time to engage in friendly conversations. Visitors are welcomed with open arms, and locals are often eager to share stories, traditions, and insights about their way of life.

Communal Spirit

Nicaragua's sense of community is palpable, with neighbors often coming together for mutual support and celebrations. Shared events, such as town fairs and religious processions, foster connections that transcend individual boundaries and emphasize the importance of unity.

Traditional Cuisine

Nicaraguan cuisine reflects the nation's diverse cultural influences. Traditional dishes like gallo pinto, nacatamal, and vigorón are enjoyed not only for their flavors but also for the sense of heritage they evoke. Sharing meals is a communal experience that brings families and friends together.

Language and Communication

Spanish is the official language of Nicaragua, and locals greatly appreciate visitors who attempt to communicate in their language. Even a few phrases or greetings in Spanish can enhance interactions and foster cultural exchange.

Eco-Consciousness

Nicaragua's connection to nature is evident in its eco-friendly practices and awareness of environmental sustainability. Many communities emphasize the importance of preserving natural resources and ecosystems for future generations.

Tips for Embracing Nicaraguan Traditions and Customs

- Respect and Openness: Approach local traditions and customs with respect, curiosity, and an open heart. Show genuine interest in learning about their significance.
- Participation: If invited to participate in a cultural event or celebration, consider joining to experience the traditions firsthand and engage with the community.
- Cultural Etiquette: Observe and follow local customs, such as greetings, during your interactions with residents to show cultural sensitivity.
- Local Guides: Engage with local guides and community members to gain deeper insights into traditions, history, and local life.
- Craft Workshops: Participate in workshops led by artisans to learn about traditional craft techniques and create your unique piece.

Festivals and Events

Nicaragua's cultural tapestry is woven with a vibrant array of festivals, artistic expressions, and intricate handicrafts that reflect the nation's history, beliefs, and creative spirit. From colorful festivals that ignite the streets with music and dance to the skillful hands that craft intricate textiles and ceramics, immersing in Nicaragua's culture is an exploration of creativity, community, and tradition. In this comprehensive guide, we'll delve into the festivals and events that pulse with energy, the world of arts and handicrafts that bear the mark of skilled artisans, and the rich cultural landscape that captures the essence of Nicaragua.

Fiestas Patronales

A tapestry of color and rhythm, Fiestas Patronales are town festivals that honor patron saints with vibrant processions, music, dancing, and religious rituals. These celebrations serve as a bridge between faith and community, bringing together locals and visitors to revel in a shared heritage. Streets come alive with parades, traditional costumes, and culinary delights, fostering a sense of unity and camaraderie.

Semana Santa (Holy Week)

Semana Santa is a spiritual and cultural highlight, marked by profound religious observances and elaborate processions that reenact the Passion of Christ. Intricately designed sawdust carpets line the streets, depicting religious scenes, while participants dressed as biblical characters lend an immersive atmosphere to the celebrations. The fusion of devotion, artistry, and tradition during Semana Santa offers a unique window into Nicaragua's cultural soul.

Palo de Mayo Festival

This Afro-Caribbean-inspired festival is a lively celebration of dance, music, and culture. Palo de Mayo, held in May, features exuberant performances characterized by vibrant costumes, rhythmic beats, and energetic dances. The festival's roots intertwine indigenous, African, and Spanish influences, creating a captivating display of multicultural heritage.

La Purísima

In November, Nicaragua comes alive with the celebration of La Purísima, which pays homage to the Virgin Mary. Elaborate altars adorned with flowers, candles, and religious images grace homes and churches. The tradition of "a la Griteria" invites locals and visitors to sing hymns, share treats, and offer prayers, fostering a sense of community and spiritual connection.

Día de la Independencia

September 15th marks Nicaragua's Independence Day, a time of patriotic pride and spirited festivities. Parades, music performances, and cultural displays showcase the nation's history and resilience, allowing both residents and visitors to join in the celebration.

Artisan Fairs and Markets

Throughout the year, artisan fairs and markets showcase the craftsmanship and creativity of local artisans. These events provide opportunities to witness the making of traditional crafts, purchase unique souvenirs, and engage with the artists themselves.

Arts and Handicrafts

Traditional Textiles

Nicaragua's textiles are a canvas of indigenous heritage and artistic skill. Handwoven fabrics, often featuring intricate patterns and vibrant colors, adorn clothing, bags, and home décor. Traditional techniques, such as the backstrap loom, are passed down through generations, preserving cultural identity through threads of artistry.

Pottery and Ceramics

The art of pottery in Nicaragua is a testament to ancestral techniques and creative innovation. Handcrafted pottery ranges from functional pieces like plates and cups to intricate sculptures and decorative items. Villages like San Juan de Oriente are known for their mastery of ceramics, with artists infusing each piece with cultural symbolism.

Woodcarvings

Woodcarving is a revered craft that captures the essence of Nicaragua's cultural diversity. Intricate sculptures, masks, and figurines are carved from hardwoods and celebrate both indigenous heritage and religious narratives. The craft's spiritual and aesthetic significance is evident in items used during traditional dances and rituals.

Hammocks and Weaving

The art of weaving extends to hammocks, a quintessential element of Nicaraguan life. Hammocks are crafted using durable fibers and intricate patterns, providing both comfort and cultural value. Weaving techniques are also evident in other items such as bags, baskets, and mats.

Paintings and Visual Arts

Nicaraguan artists express their creativity through paintings, murals, and visual arts that convey social, political, and cultural themes. Murals in cities like León and Granada narrate stories of history and identity, while contemporary artists explore modern perspectives through their canvases.

Music and Dance

Music and dance are integral to Nicaragua's cultural fabric, reflecting both indigenous and colonial influences. Marimba music resonates with ancestral rhythms, while traditional dances like the "Gigantona" and "Enano Cabezón" symbolize historical epochs. Modern genres like reggaeton and hip-hop showcase Nicaragua's evolving cultural expressions.

Literature and Poetry

Nicaragua's literary tradition is rich and enduring, with poets like Rubén Darío contributing to the nation's cultural legacy. The written word captures the nation's history, struggles, and aspirations, offering insights into its collective consciousness.

Murals and Street Art

Nicaragua's streets are adorned with vibrant murals and street art that convey societal messages and celebrate cultural identity. Murals in cities like Managua and León serve as artistic expressions of history, social commentary, and unity.

Tips for Engaging with Nicaragua's Festivals, Arts, and Handicrafts

- Attend Local Events: Seek out local festivals, markets, and celebrations to witness traditional performances, music, and crafts in their cultural context.

- Engage with Artisans: Visit artisan workshops and studios to meet the talented craftsmen and women behind the creations. Engaging in conversations with artists provides insight into their creative process and cultural inspirations.
- Respect Intellectual Property: When purchasing crafts or artwork, respect intellectual property rights and the artist's creative contributions by purchasing authentic and original pieces.
- Learn About Symbolism: Take the time to learn about the symbolism and cultural significance behind various crafts, textiles, and artistic expressions. This enhances your appreciation for their value.
- Support Sustainable Practices: When purchasing handicrafts, prioritize items made using sustainable and eco-friendly practices that preserve natural resources and support local communities.

By embracing Nicaragua's celebrations, creations, and artistic endeavors, you join a legacy of appreciating the beauty, diversity, and resilience that define the nation's cultural identity.

Culinary Experiences

Nicaragua's cultural immersion extends to the palate and the language. From the flavors of traditional cuisine that reflect the nation's history to the opportunity to learn Spanish in an authentic environment, travelers can embark on a sensory and linguistic journey that deepens their connection to the heart of Nicaragua. In this comprehensive guide, we'll explore the culinary experiences that tantalize taste buds and the benefits of learning Spanish in Nicaragua, enhancing cultural engagement and understanding.

Gallo Pinto

The iconic Gallo Pinto is a staple of Nicaraguan cuisine and a beloved breakfast dish. Combining rice and red beans with onions, sweet peppers, and spices, gallo pinto is a hearty and flavorful dish often accompanied by eggs, cheese, and plantains. It's a culinary representation of Nicaragua's diverse influences and a hearty appetite.

Nacatamal

Nacatamal is a traditional dish that showcases the artistry of Nicaraguan cooking. A large tamal wrapped in banana leaves, nacatamal is stuffed with masa (corn dough), seasoned pork, rice, and vegetables. The combination of flavors and textures creates a delectable experience that's often enjoyed on special occasions.

Vigorón

Vigorón is a dish that harmoniously blends yucca, cabbage salad, and chicharrones (fried pork skin). The contrast between the starchy yucca and the tangy cabbage salad, combined with the savory crunch of chicharrones, creates a symphony of flavors that embodies Nicaragua's culinary creativity.

Indio Viejo

Indio Viejo is a hearty stew that combines shredded beef with corn masa, vegetables, and spices. The dish is cooked until the ingredients meld into a rich and flavorful consistency, representing the historical fusion of indigenous and Spanish influences.

Sopa de Queso

Sopa de Queso is a cheese soup made with cuajada cheese, corn masa, and vegetables. The dish's creamy texture and savory flavor offer a unique and comforting culinary experience.

Rosquillas

Rosquillas are traditional Nicaraguan cookies that come in various forms, including sweet and savory versions. These crunchy treats are often enjoyed with a cup of coffee or as a snack throughout the day.

Chicha

Chicha is a traditional corn-based beverage that has been enjoyed by indigenous communities for centuries. The fermentation process gives chicha its distinctive flavor, and it is often consumed during festivals and celebrations.

Rondón

Rondón is a dish that highlights Nicaragua's coastal influences, combining coconut milk, seafood, yucca, and other ingredients. The result is a flavorful stew that reflects the nation's connection to the ocean.

Fresh Fruit Juices

Nicaragua's tropical climate yields a variety of fresh fruits that are transformed into refreshing juices. From mango and guava to tamarind and passion fruit, sipping on these natural juices is a delightful way to experience the country's bountiful produce.

Coffee and Chocolate

Nicaragua's fertile soils produce high-quality coffee and cacao beans. Visiting coffee plantations and chocolate workshops offers the chance to learn about the cultivation and production processes while savoring the flavors of locally sourced coffee and chocolate.

Learning Spanish in Nicaragua

Authentic Language Environment

Learning Spanish in Nicaragua offers the advantage of immersion in an authentic Spanish-speaking environment. Interacting with locals, practicing day-to-day conversations, and using the language in real-life situations accelerate language acquisition.

Skilled Instructors

Nicaragua boasts language schools and institutes staffed by experienced and skilled Spanish instructors. These professionals provide tailored lessons that cater to different language proficiency levels, ensuring effective learning experiences.

Cultural Integration

Learning Spanish in Nicaragua is a gateway to understanding the nation's culture on a deeper level. By communicating with locals in their native language, travelers gain insights into customs, traditions, and values that might not be fully accessible through other means.

Practical Application

The ability to speak Spanish in Nicaragua enhances practicality and convenience. Ordering food, asking for directions, and engaging in daily activities become more seamless, allowing for a smoother travel experience.

Language Exchange

Many Nicaraguans are eager to engage in language exchange, providing travelers with opportunities to learn while sharing their language and culture. This fosters mutual understanding and enriches the learning process.

Cultural Activities

Language schools in Nicaragua often integrate cultural activities into their programs. Participating in these activities, such as cooking classes, dance lessons, and guided tours, complements language learning with cultural immersion.

Homestays

Living with a host family during language studies offers an intimate glimpse into daily Nicaraguan life. Homestays provide language learners with continuous exposure to conversational Spanish and authentic cultural experiences.

Confidence Building

Learning Spanish in an immersive environment like Nicaragua builds learners' confidence in using the language. Overcoming language barriers enhances self-assurance and encourages deeper interactions with locals.

Skill Transfer

Proficiency in Spanish acquired in Nicaragua can be transferred to other Spanish-speaking countries, broadening the potential for cross-cultural experiences and connections.

Lifelong Skill

Learning Spanish is a valuable lifelong skill that opens doors to communication, understanding, and global engagement. The cultural insights gained in Nicaragua serve as a foundation for future travels and interactions.

Tips for Savoring Culinary Experiences and Learning Spanish in Nicaragua

- Engage with Locals: Strike up conversations with locals to learn about their favorite dishes and culinary traditions. Similarly, practice Spanish by engaging in conversations with natives.
- Participate in Cooking Classes: Attend cooking classes to learn the techniques and recipes behind traditional Nicaraguan dishes. This hands-on experience deepens your appreciation for the flavors and ingredients used in the cuisine.
- Explore Local Markets: Visit local markets to sample street food, fresh produce, and artisanal products. Markets offer a sensory journey through the tastes, sights, and sounds of Nicaragua.
- Enroll in Language Schools: Research language schools and institutes that offer Spanish programs tailored to different proficiency levels. Look for those that integrate cultural activities and provide immersive learning environments.

- Cultural Respect: When engaging with culinary experiences and practicing Spanish, approach interactions with cultural sensitivity and respect for local customs and traditions.
- Practice Regularly: Embrace opportunities to use your Spanish skills daily, whether it's during mealtime conversations or while exploring the local surroundings.

By indulging in the culinary wonders and embracing the language of Nicaragua, you weave a unique tapestry of cultural understanding, personal growth, and memorable moments that resonate long after you've returned home.

5

Outdoor Adventures in Nicaragua (Exploring Hiking and Trekking Routes)

Nicaragua's diverse landscape offers outdoor enthusiasts a playground of natural beauty and adventure. From dense forests to serene lakeshores, the country's hiking and trekking routes provide an opportunity to immerse oneself in its stunning scenery and connect with the raw essence of nature. In this comprehensive guide, we'll explore the hiking and trekking routes in Nicaragua that take you beyond the beaten path, allowing you to discover hidden gems, encounter wildlife, take a deep breath, and enjoy the fresh air of nature.

Hiking and Trekking Routes

Miraflor Natural Reserve

Tucked away in the northern highlands, Miraflor Natural Reserve is a haven for nature lovers and hikers seeking tranquility. The reserve offers a network of trails that wind through cloud forests, farmland, and local communities. As you explore, you'll encounter waterfalls, bird species, and lush landscapes that provide a glimpse into Nicaragua's rural life.

Nicaragua Travel Guide

Peñas Blancas Massif

For those seeking a rugged and challenging trek, the Peñas Blancas Massif delivers an immersive experience. This mountainous region boasts trails that meander through dense rainforests and ascend to panoramic viewpoints. The diversity of flora and fauna is captivating, with opportunities to spot howler monkeys, agoutis, and a variety of bird species.

Reserva Natural Tisey-Estanzuela

Located near Estelí, this reserve is a hidden gem for nature enthusiasts. Trails lead you through a mosaic of landscapes, from cloud forests and natural springs to caves adorned with stalactites. The scenic beauty is complemented by the chance to learn about the region's biodiversity and conservation efforts.

Ometepe Island Trails

The twin volcanoes of Ometepe Island, Concepción and Maderas, offer more than just their summits for exploration. The island boasts a network of trails that traverse forests, archaeological sites, and volcanic landscapes. Trails lead to the San Ramón Waterfall, Charco Verde nature reserve, and the ancient petroglyphs of Finca Magdalena.

Selva Negra Cloud Forest Reserve

This ecological treasure in the Matagalpa region presents a unique blend of cloud forests and coffee plantations. Trails guide you through dense vegetation, where you can spot various bird species, including toucans and motmots. The reserve's commitment to sustainability and eco-tourism enhances the immersive experience.

Tiscapa Lagoon Natural Reserve

Situated in the heart of Managua, Tiscapa Lagoon offers urban hikers a scenic escape. Trails wind through forests, providing a serene setting for walking, jogging, and birdwatching. The reserve also offers an observation deck that overlooks the lagoon and the cityscape, creating a harmonious balance between nature and urbanity.

Los Guatuzos Wildlife Refuge

For a unique trekking experience, explore the waterways and wetlands of Los Guatuzos Wildlife Refuge. The refuge can be navigated by boat, offering the chance to observe crocodiles, caimans, monkeys, and a plethora of bird species. Trails lead through dense foliage and along water channels, revealing the rich biodiversity of the region.

Toma de Agua Nature Reserve

Nestled in the Jinotega department, this reserve features trails that guide you through a landscape of streams, waterfalls, and diverse ecosystems. The highlight is the Toma de Agua Waterfall, where you can take a refreshing dip and relish the beauty of the cascading waters.

Chocoyero-El Brujo Natural Reserve

This protected area is a haven for bird enthusiasts and nature lovers. The reserve is home to the Pacific Green Parakeet, which nests in the chocoyero (cliffs) alongside a beautiful waterfall. Trails lead you through lush forests, offering the opportunity to spot various bird species and enjoy the sight and sound of the cascades.

Laguna de Apoyo Crater Lake

The serene beauty of Laguna de Apoyo makes it an ideal spot for a leisurely lakeside hike. The crater lake is surrounded by lush vegetation and offers trails that provide panoramic views of the water. You can also cool off with a swim in the crystal-clear waters.

Tips for Exploring Hiking and Trekking Routes in Nicaragua

- Research and Preparation: Before embarking on any hiking or trekking adventure, research the trail, its difficulty level, and the necessary permits. Make sure you're adequately prepared with proper gear, clothing, and supplies.
- Local Guides: Consider hiring a local guide for more remote trails, especially those in natural reserves. Local guides offer insights into the flora, fauna, and cultural significance of the area.
- Responsible Trekking: Follow Leave No Trace principles by minimizing your impact on the environment. Stay on designated trails, avoid disturbing wildlife, and carry out all trash.
- Weather Awareness: Nicaragua's weather can be unpredictable, especially in rainforest areas. Be prepared for changes in weather conditions and carry rain gear and appropriate clothing.

- Physical Fitness: Evaluate the physical demands of the trail and choose routes that match your fitness level. This guarantees a pleasurable and secure experience.
- Hydration and Nutrition: Carry sufficient water and snacks to stay hydrated and energized during your trek. High-energy snacks like nuts, trail mix, and fruits are ideal.
- Safety Precautions: Inform someone about your trekking plans and estimated return time. Carry a map, compass, and first aid kit, and be aware of your surroundings at all times.
- Wildlife Etiquette: If you encounter wildlife, maintain a respectful distance and avoid feeding or touching animals. Observing from a distance minimizes stress on wildlife.

As you journey through these paths less traveled, you'll encounter the heartbeats of nature, witness stunning vistas, and connect with the land in a profound way. By embracing the call of the wild and venturing into Nicaragua's great outdoors, you create memories that echo the beauty and authenticity of nature's unspoiled charm.

Volcano Exploration Adventures (Unveiling Nature's Fiery Power)

Nicaragua's landscape is marked by the presence of numerous volcanoes, offering a unique opportunity for outdoor enthusiasts and adventure seekers to engage in exhilarating volcano exploration. From climbing active peaks to gazing into smoldering craters, the country's volcanic wonders provide a one-of-a-kind adventure that combines geological marvels with breathtaking vistas. In this comprehensive guide, we'll dive into the world of volcano exploration in Nicaragua, highlighting the most iconic volcanic destinations, the experiences they offer, and the considerations for a safe and memorable adventure.

Masaya Volcano

Known as the "Mouth of Hell," Masaya Volcano is one of the most accessible active volcanoes in the world. The Santiago Crater emits a constant plume of smoke and gases, creating a surreal and otherworldly atmosphere. The ascent to the rim provides a chance to witness the impressive lava lake within the crater, best observed during nighttime for an ethereal glow.

Telica Volcano

Telica Volcano's rugged beauty and accessibility make it a popular destination for volcano exploration. The challenging hike to the summit reveals stunning views of the surrounding landscape, as well as the opportunity to peer into the volcanic crater and witness smoldering vents emitting gas and steam.

Cerro Negro Volcano

Cerro Negro's unique black sand slopes beckon adventurers to its summit. The relatively short hike is rewarded with panoramic views of neighboring volcanoes and the surrounding countryside. The real thrill comes with sandboarding down the volcanic slopes, an exhilarating experience that combines adventure with adrenaline.

Concepción and Maderas on Ometepe Island

Ometepe Island's twin volcanoes, Concepción and Maderas, present distinct exploration opportunities. The strenuous hike to Volcán Concepción's summit offers sweeping vistas of the island and Lake Nicaragua. Volcán Maderas provides a more leisurely trek through dense rainforests, culminating in a crater lake swim.

San Cristóbal Volcano

San Cristóbal is Nicaragua's highest volcano and features an impressive volcanic complex. The climb to its summit traverses through a variety of ecosystems, from tropical rainforests to barren landscapes near the summit. The final ascent rewards hikers with panoramic views and a sense of accomplishment.

Momotombo Volcano

The symmetrical cone of Momotombo Volcano rises majestically from the shores of Lake Managua. Hiking to the summit requires stamina and determination, but the views of the lake and the surrounding plains are well worth the effort. The contrast between the lush lowlands and the barren upper slopes is captivating.

Masaya Volcano National Park

This park encompasses both the Masaya Volcano and the Nindirí and Apoyo Lagoon craters. Guided tours take visitors to the active Santiago Crater, where they can peer into the smoky abyss. The park also offers opportunities to learn about the volcanic processes and the flora and fauna that thrive in this unique environment.

Volcano Boarding

For the ultimate adrenaline rush, consider volcano boarding down the slopes of Cerro Negro or other volcanic peaks. Equipped with specially designed boards, adventurers can reach speeds of up to 50 miles per hour while descending the volcanic slopes. It's an exhilarating experience that combines adventure and thrill.

Safety Precautions and Considerations

- Local Guides: When exploring volcanoes, especially those with active craters, it's advisable to hire local guides. They possess knowledge of the terrain, weather conditions, and safety protocols, enhancing your overall experience.
- Volcanic Activity: Stay informed about the status of volcanic activity before embarking on an exploration. Some volcanoes may be temporarily closed due to increased activity or safety concerns.
- Fitness Level: Many volcano hikes require a good level of physical fitness and stamina. Assess your own capabilities and choose hikes that match your experience and comfort level.
- Gear and Equipment: Wear appropriate footwear, clothing, and gear for volcano exploration. Sun protection, sturdy hiking shoes, a hat, and ample water are essential.
- Environmental Responsibility: Follow "Leave No Trace" principles to minimize your impact on the environment. Avoid disturbing wildlife and plants, and adhere to designated trails.
- Weather Awareness: Nicaragua's weather can be unpredictable. Pack clothing for various weather conditions, including rain gear and warmer layers for higher elevations.
- Permits and Regulations: Some volcanoes may require permits or entrance fees. Check-in advance and ensure you're aware of any regulations or guidelines for exploration.
- Acclimatization: If you're planning to hike higher volcanoes, consider acclimatizing to higher altitudes first to prevent altitude sickness.
- Group Travel: Exploring volcanoes with a group can enhance safety and provide a more enjoyable experience. Additionally,

group travel may offer opportunities for shared transportation and costs.

As you embark on these daring adventures, you'll not only forge unforgettable memories but also gain a deeper appreciation for the intricate relationship between the Earth's crust and the forces that shape it.

Water Sports and Surfing (Riding the Swells of the Pacific)

Nicaragua's Pacific coastline, with its pristine beaches and consistent waves, beckons water sports enthusiasts and surfers from around the world. From the thrill of catching the perfect wave to the serenity of gliding through calm waters, the country's water sports scene offers an exhilarating and rejuvenating experience for all levels of adventurers. In this comprehensive guide, we'll dive into the world of water sports and surfing in Nicaragua, exploring the diverse range of activities that allow you to immerse yourself in the ocean's embrace and embrace the coastal beauty.

Surfing

Nicaragua's Pacific coastline is a surfer's paradise, boasting consistent waves and a variety of breaks to suit all skill levels. Here are some of the best surfing spots that draw enthusiasts from around the world:

- San Juan del Sur: This vibrant coastal town offers multiple surf breaks catering to different skill levels. From the beginner-friendly beach breaks of Playa Remanso to the more challenging reef breaks of Playa Maderas and Playa Hermosa, San Juan del Sur has something for everyone.

- Popoyo: Known for its powerful waves and consistent swells, Popoyo is a top destination for experienced surfers. The area offers both beach breaks and reef breaks, creating opportunities for exhilarating rides.
- Playa Santana: With its long sandy beach and a mix of beach breaks and reef breaks, Playa Santana is a favorite among both beginners and advanced surfers. The consistent waves and friendly atmosphere make it a great place to improve your skills.
- Astillero: For those seeking a more secluded surfing experience, Astillero offers uncrowded breaks and the chance to ride waves with fewer people around. The waves here can be challenging, making it ideal for intermediate to advanced surfers.
- Playa Colorado: Accessible via the Hacienda Iguana community, Playa Colorado is famous for its hollow barrels and powerful waves. The reef break at Playa Colorado provides a thrilling challenge for experienced surfers.

Stand-Up Paddleboarding (SUP)

The calm waters of Nicaragua's coastal lagoons and serene lakes provide the perfect setting for stand-up paddleboarding. Whether you're exploring the estuaries of Juan Venado Island or gliding across the tranquil waters of Laguna de Apoyo, SUP offers a peaceful and scenic water experience.

Kayaking

Kayaking enthusiasts can explore Nicaragua's coastline, lagoons, and rivers. Paddle through the mangroves of Juan Venado Island, navigate the estuaries of La Flor Wildlife Refuge, or venture out into the pristine waters of Lake Nicaragua.

Snorkeling and Scuba Diving

Beneath the waves, a world of underwater wonders awaits. Nicaragua's coastal areas offer snorkeling and scuba diving opportunities to explore vibrant coral reefs, diverse marine life, and even the remnants of sunken ships. Popular spots include Corn Islands, Little Corn Island, and San Juan del Sur.

Sport Fishing

The waters off Nicaragua's coast are teeming with marine life, making it a prime destination for sport fishing. Whether you're after sailfish, marlin, tuna, or mahi-mahi, charter fishing trips offer the chance to reel in impressive catches while enjoying the ocean breeze.

Kiteboarding and Windsurfing

The consistent winds that sweep along Nicaragua's coastlines create ideal conditions for kiteboarding and windsurfing. Kiteboarders can catch air and perform tricks, while windsurfers can glide gracefully across the water, all against the backdrop of stunning coastal landscapes.

Jet Skiing and Water Jetpacks

For those seeking high-octane thrills, jet skiing and water jetpack experiences are available in various coastal towns. Speed across the waves or soar above the water with a water jetpack, combining adrenaline and scenic views.

Sailing

The tranquil waters of Lake Nicaragua offer an excellent setting for sailing. Rent a sailboat or join a guided sailing tour to explore the lake's islands, including the picturesque Ometepe Island with its twin volcanoes.

Whale Watching

During the migration seasons, Nicaragua's Pacific coast becomes a prime spot for whale watching. Humpback whales can often be spotted breaching and tail-slapping as they make their journey along the coast.

Eco-Tours

Combine adventure with education by joining eco-tours that explore Nicaragua's coastal ecosystems, including mangroves, estuaries, and wildlife habitats. Guided tours provide insights into the delicate balance of these environments and their importance for marine life.

Tips for Enjoying Water Sports and Surfing in Nicaragua

- Safety First: Prioritize safety by wearing appropriate gear, such as life jackets and surf leashes. Be aware of your surroundings, weather conditions, and ocean currents.
- Respect Marine Life: When snorkeling or diving, observe marine life from a respectful distance and avoid touching or disturbing underwater creatures.
- Responsible Tourism: Follow eco-friendly practices by avoiding the use of single-use plastics and respecting the

101

natural environment. Leave no trace and ensure that your presence has minimal impact on the ecosystem.

- Local Knowledge: Engage with local instructors and guides who have a deep understanding of the area's waters, currents, and conditions. Their expertise enhances your safety and overall experience.
- Skill Level: Choose water sports and surfing activities that match your skill level. Beginners should start with lessons and guided experiences to build confidence and competence.
- Environmental Awareness: Be mindful of sensitive marine habitats, such as coral reefs and mangroves. Avoid stepping on or touching these fragile ecosystems.

By immersing yourself in the world of water sports and surfing in Nicaragua, you embark on a journey that blends adventure, appreciation for marine life, and the sheer joy of riding the swells of the Pacific.

Wildlife Encounters (A Glimpse into Nicaragua's Biodiversity)

Nicaragua's diverse landscapes, from lush rainforests to tranquil lakeshores, provide a thriving habitat for a rich variety of wildlife species. For nature enthusiasts and adventure seekers alike, the country offers a unique opportunity to witness and connect with the wonders of the animal kingdom. From vibrant birds and elusive mammals to mesmerizing marine life, the wildlife encounters in Nicaragua allow you to immerse yourself in the natural beauty and biodiversity of the region. In this comprehensive guide, we'll delve into the world of wildlife encounters in Nicaragua, exploring the habitats, species, and experiences that await those who yearn to witness nature's marvels up close.

Bird Watching

Nicaragua is a paradise for bird enthusiasts, offering a diverse array of avian species. The country's varied ecosystems provide habitats for both resident and migratory birds. Some of the best bird-watching spots include:

- Juan Venado Island: This protected area is a haven for coastal and mangrove bird species. From herons and egrets to pelicans and ibises, the island's estuaries and wetlands are a birdwatcher's dream.
- Indio Maíz Biological Reserve: As one of Central America's largest rainforests, Indio Maíz is home to an astonishing variety of birdlife. Toucans, parrots, trogons, and tanagers are just a few of the species you might encounter.
- Mombacho Volcano: The cloud forests of Mombacho provide habitat for numerous bird species, including the resplendent quetzal, Nicaragua's national bird. Binoculars in hand, you can explore the canopy in search of these colorful treasures.
- Bosawás Biosphere Reserve: This expansive reserve is a UNESCO World Heritage Site and offers a haven for elusive and endangered species like the harpy eagle. Bird-watching tours here offer a chance to witness rare and unique species.
- Estero Padre Ramos: This estuary and mangrove ecosystem is another hotspot for bird watching. Waders, shorebirds, and waterfowl thrive in this biodiverse environment.

Sea Turtle Nesting

Nicaragua's beaches provide nesting sites for several species of sea turtles, making it a prime destination for witnessing this awe-inspiring natural event. Witnessing sea turtles laying their eggs and hatchlings making their way to the ocean is a truly unforgettable experience.

- La Flor Wildlife Refuge: Located on the Pacific coast, this refuge is a crucial nesting site for olive ridley and leatherback sea turtles. Guided night tours offer the chance to witness nesting and hatching activity while supporting conservation efforts.
- Playa La Flor: This remote beach within the refuge is a significant nesting site. The spectacle of hundreds of turtles coming ashore to lay their eggs during nesting season is a marvel of nature.

Mammal Watching

Nicaragua's forests and reserves are home to a variety of mammals, some of which are elusive and rare. If you have time and a keen eye, you can identify mammals like:

- Howler Monkeys: These charismatic primates are often heard before they're seen, thanks to their distinctive vocalizations. Look for troops of howler monkeys in forested areas like Mombacho and Ometepe Island.
- White-Faced Capuchin Monkeys: Capuchin monkeys are known for their playful antics and expressive faces. They can be found in certain regions, such as the cloud forests of Mombacho.
- Sloths: Nicaragua is home to two-toed and three-toed sloths, which can be spotted hanging from trees in rainforests and wooded areas. Their slow movements make them a bit of a challenge to find, but their presence is worth the effort.

- Agoutis: These rodent-like creatures can be seen scurrying through the underbrush of forests and parks. Their distinctive markings and behavior make them a fascinating sighting.
- Coatis: Coatis, also referred to as coatimundis, are raccoons. They are renowned for having long tails and being naturally curious. Watch for them in densely wooded regions.

Whale and Dolphin Watching

Nicaragua's Pacific coast offers opportunities for whale and dolphin watching, particularly during migration seasons. Witnessing these majestic marine creatures in their natural habitat is a breathtaking experience.

- El Ostional National Wildlife Refuge: Apart from sea turtles, this refuge is also frequented by humpback whales and dolphins during migration. Boat tours offer the chance to spot these marine mammals from a respectful distance.
- Corn Islands: In the waters surrounding the Corn Islands, dolphins can often be spotted riding the waves created by boats. Depending on the season, you may also have the chance to witness the migration of humpback whales.

Reptile Encounters

Nicaragua is home to a variety of reptile species, from iguanas to crocodiles. Some opportunities for reptile encounters include:

- Iguanas: Green iguanas and spiny-tailed iguanas are commonly found in forested areas, often seen basking in the sun on tree branches or rocks.

105

- Crocodiles: Certain areas, like the San Juan River, are home to populations of American crocodiles. Guided boat tours offer a safe and educational way to observe these ancient reptiles.

Butterfly and Insect Observations

Nicaragua's tropical climate fosters a vibrant population of butterflies and insects. A walk through rainforests, gardens, or even urban areas can lead to enchanting encounters with these delicate creatures.

- Montibelli Private Natural Reserve: This reserve is known for its butterfly garden, where you can witness a kaleidoscope of colors as butterflies flutter around you.

Primate Encounters

Apart from howler and capuchin monkeys, Nicaragua is also home to other primate species such as spider monkeys and squirrel monkeys. Although sightings are less common, these encounters are a testament to the country's rich biodiversity.

Tips for Enjoying Wildlife Encounters in Nicaragua

- Respectful Observation: Always observe wildlife from a respectful distance and avoid approaching or disturbing animals. Minimize noise and sudden movements to prevent stress to the creatures.
- Binoculars and Cameras: Bring binoculars and cameras with telephoto lenses to capture distant wildlife without intruding on their space.
- Local Guides: Engage local guides who are knowledgeable about the area's wildlife habitats and behaviors. Their expertise

enhances your chances of spotting animals and learning about their habits.

- Protective Gear: Wear appropriate clothing, such as neutral colors and closed-toed shoes, to minimize your impact on the environment and protect yourself from bites or stings.
- Conservation Consciousness: Support local conservation efforts by visiting eco-friendly and responsible tourism operators. Your visit can contribute to the preservation of these precious ecosystems.
- Patience: Wildlife encounters require patience. Take your time and be prepared to wait quietly for animals to emerge from their hiding spots.

Witnessing wildlife in Nicaragua isn't just about observing from a distance; it's about becoming a part of the intricate web of life that thrives in the country's diverse ecosystems. The moments when you spot a toucan perched on the treetops, a sea turtle laboring to lay her eggs, or a howler monkey calling out across the forest canopy, are reminders of the interconnectedness of all living beings and the delicate balance that sustains our planet.

As you venture into the heart of Nicaragua's natural landscapes, you embark on a journey of discovery that goes beyond the visual spectacle. Each encounter is an opportunity to learn, appreciate, and be humbled by the intricate behaviors and adaptations that have allowed these creatures to thrive in their environments. These encounters also serve as a reminder of the importance of conservation and responsible tourism, ensuring that future generations can continue to share in these awe-inspiring moments.

Whether you're an avid birder, a curious nature lover, or someone seeking a profound connection with the wild, Nicaragua's wildlife encounters promise to leave an indelible mark on your heart and soul. The memories you create, the lessons you learn, and the deep appreciation you gain for the natural world will accompany you long after you've left the country's shores. Through the lens of wildlife encounters, Nicaragua invites you to slow down, observe, and marvel at the intricate beauty that surrounds us all.

Canopy Tours and Zip Lining (Flying High Amidst Nature's Majesty)

Nicaragua's lush rainforests and breathtaking landscapes provide the perfect backdrop for a thrilling adventure that lets you experience the natural world from a whole new perspective. Canopy tours and zip lining have become popular outdoor activities in the country, offering adventurers the opportunity to soar through the treetops, witness stunning vistas, and immerse themselves in the heart of nature. In this comprehensive guide, we'll delve into the world of canopy tours and zip lining in Nicaragua, exploring the exhilarating experiences, safety considerations, and stunning destinations that await those who seek a unique adrenaline rush.

Meaning of Canopy Tours and Zip Lining

Canopy tours and zip lining provide an exciting way to explore the natural beauty of Nicaragua's rainforests, hills, and valleys. Canopy tours typically consist of a series of platforms, suspension bridges, and zip lines that allow participants to traverse through the treetops while suspended from safety harnesses. Zip lines, also known as flying foxes or zip wires, are cable-based rides that let participants glide from one platform to another at varying speeds, often offering stunning panoramic views of the surroundings.

Canopy Tours and Zip Lining Destinations

Mombacho Volcano

The cloud forests of Mombacho offer an ideal setting for canopy tours and zip lining. Traverse suspension bridges and zip lines offer breathtaking views of Lake Nicaragua, Granada, and the lush surroundings.

Ometepe Island

Zip lining on Ometepe Island provides a unique experience as you glide over lush forests, spot wildlife below, and enjoy views of the twin volcanoes. The island's diverse landscapes add an extra layer of excitement to the adventure.

San Juan del Sur

This coastal town offers canopy tours that combine zip lining with rappelling, adding an extra layer of excitement. Enjoy views of the Pacific Ocean and lush hills as you fly from platform to platform.

Estelí

The northern highlands of Estelí offer canopy tours that allow you to fly through the canopy and admire the scenic beauty of the region. It's a great way to appreciate the biodiversity of the area.

Granada

Some canopy tours in Granada offer the opportunity to zip line across the Mombacho lagoon, adding a watery twist to the adventure.

The Adventure Experience

- Adrenaline Rush: Canopy tours and zip lining provide an adrenaline rush as you glide through the air, taking in stunning views and feeling the wind rush past you.
- Spectacular Views: One of the highlights of canopy tours and zip lining is the opportunity to enjoy bird's-eye views of Nicaragua's natural beauty. From treetop vantage points to panoramic vistas, the scenery is nothing short of spectacular.
- Unique Perspective: Soaring through the canopy offers a unique perspective of the rainforest. You'll have the chance to see flora, fauna, and landscapes from a viewpoint that few get to experience.
- Connection with Nature: The immersive experience of zip lining and canopy tours allows you to feel truly connected with nature. The rustling of leaves, the calls of birds, and the smell of the forest become a part of your adventure.

Safety Considerations

- Professional Guides: Reputable canopy tour operators provide well-trained guides who are knowledgeable about the equipment, routes, and safety procedures. Follow their instructions carefully.
- Safety Gear: Participants are provided with safety gear, including harnesses, helmets, and gloves. Ensure that all equipment is properly fitted and secure before embarking on the tour.
- Weight and Age Restrictions: Some canopy tours have weight and age restrictions. It's important to adhere to these restrictions for your safety and the safety of others.

- Health Considerations: If you have certain medical conditions or physical limitations, it's essential to consult with a medical professional before participating in canopy tours or zip lining.
- Weather Conditions: Canopy tours are often weather-dependent. Tours may be canceled or rescheduled in the event of adverse weather conditions such as heavy rain or strong winds.

Responsible Tourism and Conservation

- Leave No Trace: While zip-lining and canopy tours are exhilarating, it's important to minimize your impact on the environment. Follow the principles of Leave No Trace by refraining from littering and respecting the natural surroundings.
- Support Conservation: Some canopy tour operators collaborate with local conservation organizations to support environmental protection efforts. By participating in these tours, you contribute to the preservation of Nicaragua's natural habitats.

Tips for Enjoying Canopy Tours and Zip Lining

- Dress Comfortably: Wear comfortable clothing and closed-toed shoes that allow for movement and are suitable for outdoor activities.
- Hydration: Stay hydrated before and during the tour, especially in Nicaragua's warm climate.
- Camera and Binoculars: Bring a camera or binoculars to capture the breathtaking views and wildlife you might encounter along the way.
- Reservations: Make reservations in advance, especially during peak tourist seasons, to secure your spot on the canopy tour.

- Listen to Guides: Pay close attention to the instructions provided by your guides.

As you soar through the treetops, suspended in the air and surrounded by the symphony of the rainforest, you're reminded of the incredible wonders that await when we venture beyond the ordinary and embrace the extraordinary.

From the heart of the rainforests to the heights of volcanic landscapes, Nicaragua's canopy tours and zip-lining experiences offer a new perspective on the country's rich biodiversity and awe-inspiring scenery. Whether you're seeking an adrenaline-fueled adventure or a serene encounter with nature, these activities cater to a wide range of preferences and skill levels. By participating in canopy tours and zip lining, you not only create memories that last a lifetime but also become a part of the effort to conserve and appreciate the natural treasures that make Nicaragua a truly remarkable destination.

Discovering Nicaragua's History (Unveiling the Secrets of Ancient Civilizations)

Nicaragua's history is a tapestry woven with the threads of ancient civilizations that have left behind a legacy of culture, art, and knowledge. From the intricate architecture of their cities to the stories etched in stone, the ancient civilizations that once thrived in this land continue to captivate the imagination of modern explorers. In this comprehensive guide, we'll delve into the world of Nicaragua's ancient civilizations, exploring their rise, achievements, and the echoes of their influence that can still be felt today.

The Chorotega Civilization

The Chorotega civilization, also known as the Mangue people, was one of the most prominent cultures in what is now Nicaragua. They inhabited the western part of the country, including the region around modern-day León. The Chorotega were skilled potters, and their ceramic creations featured intricate designs and depictions of animals, humans, and mythological figures.

The Chorotega people also left behind architectural remnants, including ceremonial centers and ball courts. The ball game, known as ulama, was a significant aspect of their culture and played a role in both recreation and religious rituals. While many of their structures have succumbed to the ravages of time, archaeological sites such as El Caño and Ometepe Island provide glimpses into the grandeur of their ancient settlements.

The Niquirano Civilization

The Niquirano civilization flourished in the region that encompasses modern-day Nicaragua's capital, Managua. The city of Managua is believed to have been an important hub of this civilization. Niquirano people engaged in agriculture, pottery, and trade, and their artistic expressions can still be seen in the pottery and sculptures unearthed from archaeological sites.

The Nicarao Civilization

The Nicarao civilization, from which the country derives its name, once thrived around Lake Nicaragua. These people were skilled navigators and traders, using canoes to traverse the lake's waters. They built settlements and ceremonial centers around the lake's islands and shores. The islets of Granada, located in Lake

Nicaragua, are a testament to their engineering prowess, featuring small dwellings and remnants of their ancient way of life.

The Chontales Civilization

The Chontales region in southeastern Nicaragua was inhabited by the Chontales civilization. These people are known for their metallurgical skills, particularly in working with gold. Archaeological finds include gold jewelry, figurines, and ornaments. The artistry and craftsmanship of the Chontales people speak to their cultural sophistication and artistic sensibilities.

Ometepe Island: A Microcosm of Ancient Civilizations

Ometepe Island, located in Lake Nicaragua, is a treasure trove of archaeological riches that offer insights into multiple ancient civilizations. The island is home to petroglyphs, stone carvings, and artifacts from different periods. The petroglyphs, some of which date back thousands of years, depict symbols, animals, and scenes that provide glimpses into the spiritual and cultural beliefs of these civilizations.

The Zapatera Island Petroglyphs

Zapatera Island, another island in Lake Nicaragua, is adorned with petroglyphs that reveal stories of the past. These petroglyphs depict human figures, animals, and mythological beings, offering a visual narrative of the civilization that once inhabited the island. The symbolism and intricacy of these carvings provide a window into the spiritual and cultural dimensions of ancient Nicaraguan societies.

The Legacy of Ancient Civilizations Today

The influence of Nicaragua's ancient civilizations can still be seen and felt in modern times. The artifacts, carvings, and architectural remnants that have been preserved offer a glimpse into the rich heritage that forms the foundation of the country's culture.

In various parts of Nicaragua, efforts are being made to preserve and promote the legacy of these ancient civilizations. Museums, archaeological sites, and cultural centers showcase artifacts and provide educational opportunities for locals and visitors alike to learn about the history of their land.

Visitor Experiences and Cultural Immersion

For travelers interested in exploring Nicaragua's ancient history, there are several ways to immerse themselves in the past:

- Archaeological Sites: Visit archaeological sites such as Ometepe Island, Zapatera Island, and El Caño to witness the remnants of ancient civilizations firsthand.
- Museums: Explore museums like the National Museum of Nicaragua in Managua and local museums in various cities to view artifacts and exhibits that offer insights into the ancient cultures of the region.
- Local Communities: Engage with local communities and indigenous groups to learn about their cultural heritage and the ways in which ancient traditions are still preserved.

Preservation and Cultural Heritage

Efforts are underway to ensure the preservation of Nicaragua's archaeological treasures. Collaborative projects between researchers, archaeologists, and local communities aim to safeguard these artifacts for future generations and raise awareness about the importance of cultural heritage.

Colonial Heritage (The Echoes of European Influence)

Nicaragua's colonial heritage is a reflection of the country's complex history, where the influences of indigenous cultures, European colonization, and the interplay of diverse traditions have shaped its cultural identity. From the charming cobblestone streets of colonial cities to the ornate architecture of cathedrals and fortresses, Nicaragua's colonial heritage offers a captivating journey into a bygone era. In this comprehensive guide, we will explore the colonial heritage of Nicaragua, delving into the historical context, architectural marvels, and the enduring legacy that continues to shape the nation's character.

The Arrival of the Spanish

The colonial era in Nicaragua began with the arrival of Spanish explorers and conquerors in the early 16th century. Led by figures such as Gil González de Ávila and Francisco Hernández de Córdoba, the Spanish established settlements and began the process of colonization. The Spanish influence brought about significant changes in the social, cultural, and architectural landscape of the region.

León and Granada (Rival Cities with Distinct Characters)

Two of Nicaragua's most prominent colonial cities, León and Granada, embody the duality of colonial heritage. León, established in 1524, served as Nicaragua's political and intellectual center, while Granada, founded in 1524 as well, became a hub of commerce and trade. These cities not only showcase architectural splendor but also carry within them the stories of colonial struggles and triumphs.

Architectural Marvels of Colonial Nicaragua

- Cathedrals and Churches: The cathedrals and churches of Nicaragua's colonial cities are remarkable examples of European architecture fused with indigenous craftsmanship. The León Cathedral, for instance, is known for its impressive baroque façade and intricate carvings, while Granada's Cathedral of Granada boasts neoclassical and Moorish influences.
- Convents and Monasteries: Convents and monasteries, such as the San Francisco Convent in Granada, are windows into the daily lives of colonial inhabitants. These structures served as centers of religious devotion, education, and cultural exchange.
- Fortresses and Defensive Structures: The colonial era was marked by conflicts and attempts to secure territory. Fortresses, such as the Fort of the Immaculate Conception in Rivas, were built to protect against pirate attacks and invasions. The architecture of these structures reflects the strategic importance of the region.
- Colonial Homes: Many colonial cities are adorned with well-preserved colonial homes featuring ornate balconies,

courtyards, and vibrant colors. These homes offer a glimpse into the lifestyles of colonial-era residents.

The Intricate Blend of Cultures

The colonial period in Nicaragua was characterized by the complex intermingling of European, indigenous, and African cultures. This fusion is evident in various aspects of daily life, from cuisine to language to religious practices. The blending of traditions has given rise to a unique Nicaraguan identity that is a testament to the resilience and adaptability of its people.

The Legacy of Colonial Heritage Today

The colonial heritage of Nicaragua is not confined to historical buildings and artifacts; it lives on in the traditions, customs, and cultural fabric of the nation. The influences of European architecture, religion, and language remain integral to Nicaraguan society.

Preserving and Celebrating Colonial Heritage

Efforts are underway to preserve and promote Nicaragua's colonial heritage:

- Historic Districts: Many colonial cities have designated historic districts where architectural treasures are preserved, and modern development is regulated to maintain the area's authenticity.
- Museums and Cultural Centers: Museums and cultural centers, such as the National Palace of Culture in Managua, showcase artifacts, paintings, and historical documents that shed light on the colonial era.

- Festivals and Celebrations: Traditional festivals and celebrations often incorporate elements of colonial heritage, from religious processions to cultural performances.

Visitor Experiences and Immersion

For travelers interested in delving into Nicaragua's colonial heritage, there are numerous ways to engage with the past:

- Walking Tours: Guided walking tours offer insights into the history, architecture, and stories of colonial cities. Knowledgeable guides provide context that brings the past to life.
- Cultural Festivals: Participate in cultural festivals that celebrate colonial heritage, such as Semana Santa (Holy Week), which includes processions and religious observances.
- Museums and Art Galleries: Explore museums and art galleries that exhibit colonial-era artifacts, art, and historical documents.

Revolutionary Nicaragua (Tracing the Footsteps of Liberation)

Nicaragua's history is deeply intertwined with revolutionary movements that have shaped the course of the nation's destiny. The revolutionary period, characterized by ideological struggles and grassroots movements, has left an indelible mark on the country's social, political, and cultural landscape. From the battlefields to the iconic sites that witnessed key moments of the struggle, Nicaragua's revolutionary heritage is a testament to the resilience and determination of its people. In this comprehensive guide, we will explore the revolutionary sites of Nicaragua, delving into the historical context, significant events, and the enduring legacy that continues to inspire generations.

The Sandinista Revolution

The Sandinista Revolution, which spanned from 1978 to 1990, was a pivotal period in Nicaragua's history. The revolution was led by the Sandinista National Liberation Front (FSLN), a leftist guerrilla group that sought to overthrow the authoritarian regime of Anastasio Somoza. The revolution marked a turning point in Nicaragua's trajectory, leading to social reforms, land redistribution, and efforts to address inequalities.

León (The Heart of the Revolution)

The city of León played a central role in the Sandinista Revolution. It was a stronghold of revolutionary activity and a hub of intellectual and artistic expression. León's university students were at the forefront of protests against the Somoza regime. The university's campus became a focal point for organizing demonstrations and advocating for social justice.

Monimbó (Symbol of Resistance)

The neighborhood of Monimbó in Masaya became a symbol of resistance during the revolution. In 1978, the residents of Monimbó rose against the Somoza regime, engaging in fierce battles to defend their community. The bravery of Monimbó's inhabitants captured the world's attention and became emblematic of the wider struggle for liberation.

The Battle of San Jacinto

The Battle of San Jacinto fought in 1856 during the broader struggle against foreign intervention, remains a significant milestone in Nicaragua's history. Led by General William Walker, foreign mercenaries attempted to invade Nicaragua and establish control. However, Nicaraguan forces, under the leadership of General José Dolores Estrada, emerged victorious in the Battle of San Jacinto, securing the nation's sovereignty.

Walking in the Footsteps of Heroes

- Museo de la Revolución: Located in León, the Museo de la Revolución provides an immersive experience into the Sandinista Revolution. The museum houses artifacts, photographs, and documents that chronicle the revolution's events and the lives of those who participated.
- Plaza de la Revolución: In Managua, the Plaza de la Revolución serves as a tribute to the revolutionaries who fought for freedom. The plaza features monuments, sculptures, and murals that honor the revolution's leaders and commemorates their sacrifice.
- Mausoleo de los Mártires: The Mausoleo de los Mártires (Mausoleum of the Martyrs) in León is a resting place for those who lost their lives during the Sandinista Revolution. It stands as a solemn reminder of the sacrifices made in the pursuit of justice and liberation.
- Chico Grande: The community of Chico Grande in the Matagalpa region was a sanctuary for Sandinista fighters during the revolution. The area's natural beauty and mountainous terrain provided a strategic advantage for the revolutionaries.

- La Hacienda de los Mártires: Located in Jinotepe, La Hacienda de los Mártires is a former Somoza family estate that was transformed into a training camp for Sandinista guerrillas. Today, it stands as a testament to the revolution's transformative impact.

The Enduring Legacy

The legacy of Nicaragua's revolutionary period extends beyond historical sites:

- Educational Reforms: The Sandinista government prioritized education, leading to improvements in literacy rates and access to education for marginalized communities.
- Healthcare Initiatives: Efforts were made to provide healthcare services to underserved populations, resulting in expanded healthcare access and initiatives to combat disease.
- Social and Land Reforms: The Sandinista government implemented land redistribution programs, aimed at addressing land inequalities and empowering rural communities.
- Cultural Expression: The revolution spurred artistic and cultural expression, with music, literature, and visual arts becoming mediums for conveying messages of hope, solidarity, and social change.

Preserving the Legacy

Nicaragua's revolutionary heritage is being preserved and celebrated through various initiatives:

- Education: Schools and universities integrate the history of the revolution into their curricula, ensuring that future generations understand the importance of the struggle for liberation.
- Commemorative Events: Anniversaries of key revolutionary moments are commemorated through events, exhibitions, and cultural activities.
- Oral History Projects: Efforts are made to document and preserve the firsthand accounts of individuals who participated in the revolution, ensuring that their stories are passed down to future generations.

Visitor Experiences and Immersion

For those interested in delving into Nicaragua's revolutionary heritage, there are meaningful ways to connect with the past:

- Guided Tours: Participate in guided tours that explore revolutionary sites, providing historical context and insights into the events that unfolded.
- Cultural Festivals: Attend cultural festivals that celebrate the spirit of the revolution through music, dance, and art.
- Museums and Memorials: Visit museums and memorials dedicated to the revolution, where artifacts, photographs, and documents provide a deeper understanding of the era.

As you stand in the places where revolutionaries once stood, you become a witness to history, tracing the footsteps of those who sought to reshape their nation's destiny. Nicaragua's revolutionary heritage invites us to remember, reflect, and honor the legacy of struggle that continues to inspire individuals and movements around the world. It's a reminder that the pursuit of freedom and justice is a journey that transcends time and connects us all as champions of change.

Museums and Historical Landmarks (Portals to Nicaragua's History and Culture)

Nicaragua's museums and historical landmarks offer a rich tapestry of narratives that reflect the country's diverse history, culture, and heritage. From pre-Columbian artifacts to colonial architecture, and revolutionary artifacts to contemporary art, these sites provide a window into the past, inviting visitors to explore the layers of Nicaragua's identity. In this comprehensive guide, we will embark on a journey through Nicaragua's museums and historical landmarks, delving into the stories they tell, the treasures they house, and the significance they hold for both locals and travelers.

Museo Nacional de Nicaragua

The Museo Nacional de Nicaragua, located in the capital city of Managua, serves as a repository of the nation's history, art, and culture. The museum's exhibits are organized chronologically, guiding visitors through the different periods that have shaped Nicaragua's identity. From pre-Columbian artifacts to colonial relics and revolutionary memorabilia, the museum offers a comprehensive overview of the country's heritage.

Museo de la Revolución

The Museo de la Revolución, situated in León, provides a deeply immersive experience of the Sandinista Revolution. Through artifacts, photographs, documents, and multimedia presentations, visitors gain insights into the struggle, sacrifice, and triumphs of the revolutionary period. The museum captures the spirit of the revolution and pays homage to those who fought for social justice and equality.

Cathedral of León

The Cathedral of León, a UNESCO World Heritage Site, is a remarkable example of colonial architecture. Its baroque façade and ornate interior reflect the intricate craftsmanship of the period. The cathedral also houses the remains of prominent figures from Nicaragua's history, including poet Rubén Darío. Climbing to the rooftop provides panoramic views of the city and the surrounding landscapes.

Ruins of León Viejo

León Viejo, the original site of León, was buried under volcanic ash in the 17th century. Today, the ruins of León Viejo are a UNESCO-listed site, offering a glimpse into the daily life and architecture of the colonial period. Visitors can explore the remains of churches, homes, and public buildings that once thrived in this historical settlement.

Fortaleza La Inmaculada

The Fortaleza La Inmaculada, located in the city of El Castillo, is a testament to Nicaragua's efforts to protect its territories from foreign invasions. This fortress, situated on the San Juan River, was built during the colonial era to defend against pirate attacks. The well-preserved structure offers insights into the military strategies and architectural techniques of the time.

Museo Sitio Huellas de Acahualinca

The Museo Sitio Huellas de Acahualinca, also known as the Footprints of Acahualinca Museum, is home to a unique archaeological discovery. The museum showcases ancient footprints preserved in volcanic ash, providing a glimpse into the lives of early inhabitants of the region. The footprints offer insights into the activities, movements, and interactions of these ancient communities.

Museo de Arte Fundación Ortiz-Gurdián

The Museo de Arte Fundación Ortiz-Gurdián, located in León, is a cultural gem that celebrates contemporary art. The museum's extensive collection includes works by both Nicaraguan and international artists, spanning various mediums and styles. The museum also hosts temporary exhibitions, workshops, and cultural events that contribute to León's vibrant arts scene.

Rubén Darío National Theatre

Named after Nicaragua's renowned poet, the Rubén Darío National Theatre in Managua is a cultural landmark that hosts theatrical performances, concerts, and cultural events. The theatre's architecture blends neoclassical and baroque influences, creating a captivating space that resonates with the spirit of artistic expression.

The Masaya Volcano National Park

While primarily known for its volcanic activity, the Masaya Volcano National Park also holds historical significance. It was here that indigenous people sought refuge during the Spanish

126

conquest. The park features a visitor center that provides information about the volcano's geological and cultural importance.

La Polvora Fortress

La Polvora Fortress in Granada is another historical gem that offers insights into Nicaragua's past. Built during the 18th century, the fortress served as a gunpowder magazine and defensive structure. Today, it stands as a symbol of Granada's history and resilience.

Casa de los Tres Mundos

Casa de los Tres Mundos, located in Granada, is a cultural center that promotes the arts and offers cultural programs for the community. The center hosts exhibitions, workshops, and performances, fostering artistic expression and cross-cultural understanding.

Preserving Heritage for Future Generations

Nicaragua's commitment to preserving its heritage is evident through various initiatives:

- Conservation Efforts: Many museums and historical sites implement conservation measures to ensure the preservation of artifacts, documents, and architectural structures.
- Educational Programs: Museums offer educational programs and workshops that engage visitors, especially students, in learning about Nicaragua's history and culture.
- Community Involvement: Some museums collaborate with local communities to ensure that the history and traditions of indigenous peoples are accurately represented.

Visitor Experiences and Cultural Immersion

Exploring Nicaragua's museums and historical landmarks offers unique opportunities for cultural immersion:

- Guided Tours: Engage in guided tours that provide context, stories, and insights into the historical and cultural significance of each site.
- Interactive Exhibits: Many museums offer interactive exhibits that allow visitors to engage with artifacts, documents, and multimedia presentations.
- Art Workshops: Participate in art workshops and classes hosted by cultural centers and museums to experience the creative spirit of Nicaragua.

As you walk through museum halls, stand in the shadows of ancient ruins, and marvel at the artistic expressions of contemporary artists, you become a part of the continuum of discovery and appreciation.

Each artifact, each building, and each story invites us to connect with the threads that bind us to history and culture. By engaging with Nicaragua's museums and historical landmarks, we celebrate the resilience, creativity, and spirit of a nation that continues to honor its past while embracing its future. It's a journey of exploration that allows us to unravel the layers of time and uncover the stories that have shaped Nicaragua's captivating tapestry.

6

Sustainable Travel and Responsible Tourism in Nicaragua (Nurturing Nature and Empowering Communities)

Nicaragua's allure extends beyond its natural beauty and cultural riches; it also encompasses a commitment to sustainable travel and responsible tourism. The country's ecotourism initiatives, community-based projects, and efforts to promote responsible traveler behavior exemplify Nicaragua's dedication to preserving its environment and supporting local communities. In this comprehensive guide, we will delve into the world of sustainable travel and responsible tourism in Nicaragua, exploring ecotourism endeavors, community-driven projects, and practical tips for being a responsible traveler.

Ecotourism Initiatives: Harmonizing with Nature

Ometepe Island (A Model of Ecotourism)

Ometepe Island, situated in Lake Nicaragua, stands as a prime example of ecotourism done right. The island's lush landscapes, diverse ecosystems, and sustainable practices have made it a haven for eco-conscious travelers. Visitors can engage in activities such as hiking, birdwatching, and kayaking, while local guides provide insights into the island's flora, fauna, and cultural heritage.

Bosawás Biosphere Reserve (A Biodiversity Hotspot)

Bosawás Biosphere Reserve, one of the largest protected areas in Central America, is a testament to Nicaragua's commitment to preserving its natural treasures. The reserve is home to an incredible array of species, including jaguars, tapirs, and harpy eagles. Community-led ecotourism initiatives allow travelers to explore this pristine wilderness while contributing to conservation efforts.

Estelí (Coffee and Conservation)

In the city of Estelí, sustainable travel takes on a caffeinated twist. Coffee farms in the region offer immersive experiences where travelers can learn about the coffee production process, from bean to cup. These tours highlight the importance of sustainable farming practices that protect the environment and support local communities.

Volcanoes and National Parks

Nicaragua's volcanoes and national parks provide opportunities for ecotourism and adventure. Volcano hikes, canopy tours, and wildlife spotting adventures are often conducted with a strong emphasis on environmental conservation and responsible practices.

Community-Based Projects (Empowering Locals, Enriching Experiences)

Los Ramos (Sustainable Agriculture and Cultural Immersion)

The community of Los Ramos near Granada engages in sustainable agriculture practices that align with ecotourism principles. Visitors have the chance to participate in farming activities, learn about traditional methods, and share meals with local families. The experience fosters cultural exchange and economic empowerment for the community.

El Chile (Artisan Crafts and Empowerment)

In the town of El Chile, artisans work to preserve traditional crafts while generating income for their families. Travelers can engage with the community, observe the creative process, and purchase unique handmade items. The interaction supports local livelihoods and encourages the continuation of cultural practices.

Los Maribios (Community Tourism in Action)

The Los Maribios community tourism network showcases the collaboration between local communities, tour operators, and travelers. By staying with local families, participating in cultural activities, and contributing to community development projects, travelers directly support sustainable initiatives and experience Nicaragua from an authentic perspective.

Tips for Being a Responsible Traveler

Respect Local Customs and Traditions

Understanding and respecting local customs, traditions, and etiquette contribute to cultural sensitivity and positive interactions. Learning a few phrases in Spanish can also go a long way in building connections.

Choose Eco-Friendly Accommodations

Opt for accommodations that prioritize sustainability, such as eco-lodges and hotels with green certifications. These establishments often implement practices that reduce energy consumption, minimize waste, and support local communities.

Support Local Businesses

Purchasing locally-made souvenirs, dining at local eateries, and engaging in community-based tours contribute to the economic well-being of local communities. This approach ensures that the benefits of tourism are distributed widely.

Minimize Environmental Impact

Follow the principles of "leave no trace" by minimizing your impact on natural areas. Dispose of waste responsibly, conserve water, and avoid damaging flora and fauna.

Participate in Conservation Efforts

Many destinations offer opportunities to participate in conservation activities, such as beach cleanups, tree planting, and wildlife monitoring. Contributing to these efforts supports the preservation of Nicaragua's natural beauty.

Respect Wildlife

Observe wildlife from a respectful distance and avoid disturbing animals or their habitats. Avoid activities that involve direct contact with wildlife, as these can have negative consequences.

Conserve Resources

Conserve resources such as water and electricity, especially in areas where these resources may be limited. Use reusable items like water bottles and shopping bags to minimize waste.

Seek Educational Experiences

Participate in tours and activities that provide insights into local culture, history, and environmental conservation. Learning about Nicaragua's heritage enhances your travel experience and fosters a deeper appreciation for the destination.

Spread Awareness

Share your experiences and insights with others, encouraging responsible travel practices and promoting the importance of sustainability and conservation.

Choose Responsible Tour Operators

Select tour operators that prioritize responsible tourism practices, including minimizing environmental impact, respecting local cultures, and contributing to community development.

Support Conservation Organizations

Consider donating to or volunteering with local conservation organizations that work to protect Nicaragua's natural habitats and wildlife.

Leave a Positive Footprint

Ultimately, being a responsible traveler means leaving a positive impact on the places you visit. By fostering connections, supporting communities, and nurturing the environment, you contribute to the long-term sustainability and well-being of Nicaragua and its people.

By engaging with ecotourism initiatives, supporting community-based projects, and adopting responsible traveler practices, visitors become stewards of the destination they explore. Nicaragua's efforts to harmonize tourism with conservation and community empowerment are a testament to the shared responsibility of nurturing the planet and ensuring that its treasures endure for generations to come.

7

Transportation in Nicaragua (Connecting Destinations)

Transportation in Nicaragua plays a crucial role in exploring the diverse landscapes, vibrant cities, and cultural treasures that the country has to offer. From bustling urban centers to tranquil rural areas, Nicaragua's transportation options provide travelers with a range of choices to suit their preferences and needs. In this comprehensive guide, we will delve into the practical information you need to navigate Nicaragua's transportation network, including modes of transportation, tips for getting around, and insights into local travel culture.

Domestic Flights

For travelers seeking to cover long distances quickly, domestic flights are a convenient option. Nicaragua has several domestic airports, including Managua, Granada, and San Juan del Sur. Airlines like La Costeña and Atlantic Airlines operate flights between major cities and tourist destinations, making it easier to access different regions of the country.

Buses

Buses are a popular and affordable mode of transportation in Nicaragua. They connect cities, towns, and rural areas, providing a comprehensive network that spans the country. There are two main types of buses: express buses and chicken buses. Express buses offer more comfort and convenience, while chicken buses are colorful and often more budget-friendly.

Taxis and Ride-Sharing

Taxis are readily available in urban areas and can be hailed on the street or booked through apps. Ride-sharing services like Uber operate in cities like Managua, Granada, and León, providing a convenient and reliable option for getting around.

Rental Cars

Renting a car gives you the freedom to explore Nicaragua at your own pace. Rental car agencies are available at major airports and cities. Keep in mind that road conditions may vary, and some areas may require a four-wheel-drive vehicle.

Ferries and Boats

Nicaragua's extensive network of lakes and rivers provides opportunities for ferry and boat travel. Ferries connect the mainland to islands like Ometepe and provide scenic routes between coastal towns.

Horse-Drawn Carriages and Tuk-Tuks

In some cities and towns, horse-drawn carriages and tuk-tuks offer a charming and unique way to explore. These modes of transportation are especially common in places like Granada and León.

Motorcycles and Scooters

Renting a motorcycle or scooter can be a thrilling way to navigate Nicaragua's roads. However, make sure you have the necessary experience and proper safety gear before embarking on this adventure.

Cycling

Cycling enthusiasts can explore Nicaragua's landscapes on two wheels. Many cities and towns have bike rental shops, and some areas offer dedicated cycling routes.

Traveling by Foot

Exploring on foot is a wonderful way to immerse yourself in local culture and discover hidden gems. Walking tours are available in cities like Granada and León, allowing you to explore historical sites and neighborhoods.

Tips for Navigating Nicaragua's Transportation Network

Plan Ahead

Research transportation options and schedules before your trip to ensure smooth travel between destinations.

Currency and Payments

Carry local currency (Nicaraguan córdobas) for bus fares and smaller transactions. Larger establishments may accept credit cards.

Safety Considerations

Exercise caution and be aware of your surroundings, especially when using public transportation. Keep your possessions safe, and don't show off any expensive valuables.

Language Barrier

While some transportation staff may speak English, it's helpful to know basic Spanish phrases for communication.

Ask Locals for Advice

Locals can provide valuable insights into transportation options, routes, and cultural norms. Don't hesitate to ask for recommendations.

Check for Updates

Transportation schedules and availability may change, especially in rural areas. Check for updates before embarking on your journey.

Travel Insurance

Consider purchasing travel insurance that covers transportation-related issues, such as flight delays or cancellations.

Embrace the Experience

Traveling in Nicaragua provides the opportunity to connect with locals and fellow travelers. Embrace the journey, and don't be afraid to engage in conversations and learn from the people you meet.

Traveling Responsibly and Culturally Aware

Respect Local Customs

When using public transportation, respect local customs and etiquette. Give up your seat to elders, avoid loud conversations, and follow any rules or guidelines provided.

Interact with Respect

Engage with drivers, conductors, and fellow passengers with respect and courtesy. Small gestures of kindness, such as saying "buenos días" (good morning) when boarding a bus, go a long way.

Be Patient

Transportation schedules and routes may not always be punctual or predictable. Exercise patience and flexibility, and understand that delays are part of the travel experience.

Environmental Considerations

Choose eco-friendly transportation options when possible. For example, opt for buses or shared rides over private cars to reduce carbon emissions.

Learn Basic Phrases

Learning a few basic Spanish phrases can greatly enhance your travel experience and help you communicate with transportation staff and locals.

Be Mindful of Crowds

Public transportation, especially buses, can become crowded during peak hours. Be prepared for close quarters and maintain a respectful demeanor.

Support Local Economies

When using transportation services like taxis, tuk-tuks, or horse-drawn carriages, negotiate fares fairly and avoid haggling excessively.

Participate in Local Customs

If invited, participate in local customs or practices related to transportation. For example, if locals offer to share food or engage in conversations, embrace the opportunity to connect.

Safety and Security Guidelines (Navigating Nicaragua with Caution)

When traveling to Nicaragua, prioritizing safety, security, and managing your finances are essential aspects of ensuring a smooth and enjoyable experience. Understanding local customs, being aware of potential risks, and managing your money wisely can greatly enhance your journey in this diverse and vibrant country. In this comprehensive guide, we will delve into the practical information you need to stay safe, secure, and financially savvy while exploring Nicaragua.

Research and Planning

Before your trip, conduct a thorough research about the areas you plan to visit. Understand the current safety situation, any travel advisories, and local customs. Stay informed about the political and social climate to make informed decisions.

Register with Your Embassy

Upon arrival, register with the embassy or consulate of your country. This helps them keep track of your whereabouts and enables them to reach out in case of emergencies or travel advisories.

Local Contacts

Have local contacts, such as the contact information of your hotel, tour operators, and trusted locals. This can be invaluable in case you need assistance or guidance.

Travel Insurance

Invest in thorough travel insurance that includes personal property coverage, trip cancellation protection, and medical emergencies. Make sure you understand the coverage and how to access assistance if needed.

Health Precautions

Check with your healthcare provider about recommended vaccinations before traveling to Nicaragua. Carry any necessary medications and medical supplies, and be aware of local healthcare facilities.

Avoid Isolated Areas at Night

While Nicaragua is generally safe, avoid isolated areas and poorly lit streets at night. Stick to well-lit and populated areas, and consider traveling in groups.

Petty Theft Prevention

Practice caution against petty theft. Keep your belongings secure, avoid displaying expensive items, and use money belts or concealed pouches to carry valuables.

Respect Local Customs

Understanding and respecting local customs and traditions is essential for personal safety and cultural sensitivity. Dress modestly in conservative areas and observe local practices.

Stay Hydrated

Nicaragua's tropical climate can be hot and humid. Stay hydrated by drinking lots of water, especially if you're doing outside activities.

Emergency Numbers

Know the local emergency numbers for police, medical services, and fire department. These numbers can be crucial in times of need.

Use Reputable Tour Operators

Select reliable and authorized tour operators while taking excursions or tours. Research reviews and ask for recommendations to ensure your safety.

Blend In

Avoid drawing unnecessary attention to yourself by dressing like a local and behaving respectfully. This can reduce the likelihood of becoming a target for scams or theft.

Currency Exchange

Use official currency exchange offices or banks to exchange your money. Avoid exchanging currency on the street or through unofficial channels.

Language Skills

Learn basic Spanish phrases to communicate with locals. Being able to ask for directions or assistance can be helpful in unfamiliar situations.

Currency and Money Matters (Managing Finances in Nicaragua)

Currency

The Nicaraguan córdoba (NIO) is the country of Nicaragua's national currency. Familiarize yourself with the currency's denominations and appearance before your trip.

Currency Exchange

Exchanging money can be done at banks, currency exchange offices, and some hotels. Be cautious of fluctuating exchange rates and compare rates to get the best deal.

ATM Usage

In large cities and popular tourist locations, ATMs are extensively available. Stick to ATMs at reputable banks and use caution when entering your PIN.

Credit Cards

Major credit cards are accepted in larger establishments, but it's advisable to carry cash for smaller transactions and in more remote areas.

Small Bills

Carry smaller denominations of currency for daily expenses, as larger bills may not be accepted in some places.

Tipping Etiquette

Tipping is not mandatory in Nicaragua, but it's appreciated for good service. In restaurants, leaving a small tip or rounding up the bill is customary.

Bargaining and Haggling

Bargaining is common in markets and for certain services. However, be respectful and avoid aggressive negotiation tactics.

Budget Wisely

Set a budget for your trip and track your expenses to avoid overspending. This can help you make the most of your journey without financial stress.

Scams and Counterfeit Money

Be cautious of scams involving counterfeit money. Familiarize yourself with the local currency to identify genuine notes.

Safety of Belongings

Keep your money, credit cards, and important documents secure. Consider using a money belt or pouch to prevent theft.

Local Cost of Living

Understanding the local cost of living can help you budget more effectively. Research prices for accommodations, meals, transportation, and activities.

Access to ATMs

While ATMs are available in urban areas, they may be limited in rural regions. Plan accordingly and withdraw sufficient cash in advance.

Online Banking and Security

If using online banking, ensure that your accounts are secure with strong passwords and two-factor authentication.

Keep Emergency Cash

Maintain a small emergency fund that is distinct from your regular money. This can be useful in case of unexpected situations.

Exchange Rates

Monitor exchange rates to make informed currency exchange decisions. Consider using currency conversion apps for real-time updates.

Carry a Small Calculator

Carrying a small calculator can be helpful for converting prices from córdobas to your home currency.

Avoid Flashy Displays of Wealth

Minimize displaying expensive jewelry, electronics, or large amounts of cash to avoid attracting unwanted attention.

Communication and Internet (Staying Connected in Nicaragua)

In today's interconnected world, staying connected while traveling is crucial for convenience, safety, and sharing your experiences with loved ones. When visiting Nicaragua, understanding the communication infrastructure and internet options available is essential for a seamless and enjoyable journey. From staying in touch with family and friends to navigating new destinations, this guide provides comprehensive information on communication and the internet in Nicaragua.

Mobile Networks and Providers

Nicaragua has a well-established mobile network system, making it easy to stay connected through calls and mobile data. The major mobile providers in the country include Claro, Movistar, and

CooTel. These providers offer prepaid SIM cards and various data packages that cater to different needs.

Purchasing a SIM Card

Upon arrival in Nicaragua, you can purchase a prepaid SIM card from kiosks, convenience stores, or official mobile provider shops. To do this, you'll need to present your passport and fill out some basic paperwork. The SIM card comes with a Nicaraguan phone number and can be easily inserted into your unlocked phone.

Data Packages

Mobile providers offer a range of data packages that allow you to access the internet and use apps on the go. These packages vary in terms of data volume and validity, so choose one that aligns with your usage patterns. You can recharge your account with additional data as needed.

Public Wi-Fi

Public Wi-Fi is available in many hotels, restaurants, cafes, and tourist areas. However, the quality and speed of the connection may vary. Public Wi-Fi is convenient for checking emails, social media, and light web browsing, but it may not be suitable for data-intensive activities like streaming or video calls.

Internet Cafes

Internet cafes are still present in some areas of Nicaragua, especially in smaller towns and rural locations. These cafes provide access to computers and the internet for a fee. If you need

Nicaragua Travel Guide

to use a computer or require a stable internet connection, internet cafes can be a viable option.

Communication Apps

Using communication apps on your mobile device can be an efficient way to stay connected with family and friends back home. Apps like WhatsApp, Skype, Viber, and Facebook Messenger allow you to make voice and video calls over the Internet, reducing the need for international calling plans.

Roaming Charges

Before using your home country's SIM card in Nicaragua, be aware of potential roaming charges. International roaming can be expensive, so it's recommended to switch to a local SIM card or use Wi-Fi whenever possible.

Local Phone Calls

Making local phone calls within Nicaragua is straightforward. Dial the local area code followed by the seven-digit phone number. If you're calling a mobile number, you'll need to add the mobile provider's prefix before the number.

Emergency Services

The emergency number for police, medical services, and fire department in Nicaragua is 911. Make sure you know this number and have access to a working phone in case of emergencies.

Internet Reliability

While urban areas typically have reliable internet connectivity, more remote or rural regions may have intermittent or slower internet access. Plan accordingly if you require a consistent internet connection for work or communication.

Virtual Private Networks (VPNs)

If you're concerned about online privacy and security, consider using a VPN when accessing public Wi-Fi networks. VPNs encrypt your internet traffic, protecting your data from potential hackers or eavesdroppers.

Local Communication Norms

When communicating with locals, politeness and respect are valued. Address people using appropriate titles (Mr., Mrs., etc.) and use courteous phrases such as "buenos días" (good morning) and "por favor" (please).

Internet for Travel Planning

The internet is a valuable tool for planning your itinerary, finding accommodation, researching attractions, and getting directions. Utilize online maps and travel forums to gather information before and during your trip.

Keeping Loved Ones Updated

Using communication apps and social media platforms, keep your family and friends updated about your travels and experiences. Sharing photos and stories can enhance your connection and provide them with a glimpse into your journey.

Whether you're sending a message to loved ones or using the internet to explore new destinations, Nicaragua's digital landscape empowers you to make the most of your journey while staying connected with the world.

Essential Phrases in Spanish (Bridging Cultural and Linguistic Gaps)

When traveling to Nicaragua, having a basic understanding of Spanish can greatly enhance your experience and interactions with locals. While many Nicaraguans in the tourism industry may speak English, knowing a few essential Spanish phrases can go a long way in connecting with the culture, navigating daily situations, and showing respect to the people you encounter. In this comprehensive guide, we will provide you with a list of essential Spanish phrases tailored for travelers exploring Nicaragua, along with insights into pronunciation and usage.

Greetings and Basic Phrases

- Hola - Hello
- Buenos días - Good morning
- Buenas tardes - Good afternoon
- Buenas noches - Good evening/night
- Por favor - Please
- Gracias - Thank you
- De nada - You're welcome
- Perdón - Excuse me
- Lo siento - I'm sorry

Introductions

- Cómo te llamas? - What's your name?

Asking for Help and Directions

- Dónde está...? - Where is...?
- Cómo llego a...? - How do I get to...?
- Necesito ayuda - I need help
- Habla inglés? - Do you speak English?

Ordering Food and Drinks

- Una mesa para [number of people] - A table for [number of people]
- Quisiera... - I would like...
- La cuenta, por favor - The bill, please
- Qué recomiendas? - What do you recommend?
- Agua - Water
- Cerveza - Beer
- Vino - Wine
- Café - Coffee
- Té - Tea

Shopping and Bargaining

- Cuánto cuesta? - How much does it cost?
- Puede hacer un descuento? - Can you give me a discount?
- Me gusta, lo voy a llevar - I like it, I'll take it

Transportation

- Cuánto cuesta el boleto? - How much is the ticket?
- A dónde va este autobús? - Where does this bus go?
- Cuánto es el taxi a...? - How much is the taxi to...?

Numbers and Currency

- Diez, veinte, treinta, cuarenta, cincuenta - Ten, twenty, thirty, forty, fifty
- Cien - One hundred
- Mil - One thousand
- Cuánto cuesta en córdobas/dólares? - How much is it in córdobas/dollars?

Cultural Etiquette

- Puedo sacar una foto? - Can I take a photo?
- Está bien si...? - Is it okay if...?
- Respeto - Respect

Getting to Know Locals

- De dónde eres? - Where are you from?
- Me encanta Nicaragua - I love Nicaragua
- Puedo aprender más sobre tu cultura? - Can I learn more about your culture?

Pronunciation Tips

Spanish pronunciation is generally straightforward, with each letter corresponding to a specific sound. Here are some basic tips:

- C is pronounced like "k" when before a, o, or u (e.g., casa - "kah-sah").
- C is pronounced like "s" when before e or i (e.g., cerveza - "ser-veh-sah").
- G is pronounced like "h" when before e or i (e.g., gente - "hen-te").

- J is pronounced like the Scottish "ch" in "loch" (e.g., jefe - "he-fe").
- LL is pronounced like "y" in "yes" (e.g., calle - "ka-yeh").
- Ñ is pronounced like "ny" (e.g., niño - "nee-nyoh").
- R is rolled (e.g., río - "ree-oh").

Mastering these essential Spanish phrases will empower you to engage more deeply with the culture and people of Nicaragua. While the phrases provided cover common situations, don't hesitate to learn more as you explore and interact. Nicaraguans appreciate the effort, and your willingness to connect through language will undoubtedly lead to memorable and enriching experiences during your travels.

8

Sample Itineraries (Exploring Nicaragua's Treasures)

Nicaragua, with its diverse landscapes, rich history, and vibrant culture, offers a range of experiences for every type of traveler. From adventure enthusiasts to culture seekers and families, Nicaragua has something to offer to all. In this comprehensive guide, we will curate sample itineraries for different types of travelers, ensuring that your journey through Nicaragua is both enriching and unforgettable. Whether you have one week, or two weeks, or are traveling with your family, these sample itineraries will guide you through the best that Nicaragua has to offer.

One-Week Nicaragua Adventure

Day 1 (Arrival in Managua)

- Arrive at Augusto C. Sandino International Airport in Managua.
- Transfer to your accommodation and relax after your flight.
- Explore Managua's historic sites like the Old Cathedral and the National Palace of Culture.

Day 2 (Volcano Adventure)

- Depart for León, known for its colonial charm and nearby volcanoes.
- Hike up Cerro Negro, an active volcano, and experience volcano boarding.
- Visit the vibrant local market and enjoy authentic Nicaraguan cuisine.

Day 3 (León Exploration)

- Explore the colonial architecture of León, including the UNESCO-listed Cathedral of León.
- Visit the Museo de la Revolución to learn about Nicaragua's history.
- Enjoy an evening at a local café or bar, soaking in the city's artistic vibe.

Day 4 (Tranquil Beaches of Las Peñitas)

- Travel to Las Peñitas, a coastal village known for its relaxed atmosphere.
- Enjoy beach activities like surfing, swimming, and beachfront yoga.
- Savor fresh seafood and stunning sunsets over the Pacific Ocean.

Day 5 (San Juan del Sur)

- Head south to San Juan del Sur, a popular beach town.
- Explore local shops, art galleries, and relax on the golden sands.

- Experience the town's vibrant nightlife with beachfront parties and live music.

Day 6 (Adventure and Relaxation)

- Engage in water sports like kayaking or stand-up paddleboarding.
- Take a boat tour to spot dolphins and enjoy the coastal views.
- Indulge in a relaxing beachside massage or spa treatment.

Day 7 (Farewell to Nicaragua)

- Spend your final morning by the beach, reflecting on your journey.
- Transfer back to Managua for your departure flight.

Two-Week Cultural Immersion

Day 1-3 (Managua and Granada)

- Arrive in Managua and explore the capital's historical and cultural sites.
- Travel to Granada, a colonial gem known for its colorful streets and architecture.
- Visit the Mi Museo art gallery and experience a traditional dance performance.

Day 4-6 (Ometepe Island)

- Take a ferry to Ometepe Island and immerse yourself in its natural beauty.
- Explore the island's hiking trails, waterfalls, and petroglyphs.
- Learn about local traditions and enjoy farm-to-table meals.

Day 7-9 (Masaya and Markets)

- Visit Masaya, known for its artisan markets and an active volcano.
- Explore the Masaya Crafts Market and purchase unique souvenirs.
- Attend a traditional dance performance and savor local cuisine.

Day 10-12 (León and Cultural Heritage)

- Travel to León and discover its colonial history and revolutionary past.
- Explore the city's art galleries, murals, and bustling markets.
- Take a guided walking tour to learn about León's architectural and cultural heritage.

Day 13-14 (San Juan del Sur and Beach Bliss)

- Relax in San Juan del Sur, enjoying beach activities and the local scene.
- Visit nearby beaches like Playa Hermosa and Playa Maderas.
- Participate in a cooking class to learn how to prepare Nicaraguan dishes.

Family-Friendly Vacation Ideas

Day 1-3 (Managua and Family Fun)

- Arrive in Managua and settle into family-friendly accommodations.
- Visit the Montoya Family Park, an amusement park with rides and attractions.

- Explore the Children's Museum of Managua, offering interactive exhibits.

Day 4-6 (Granada and Adventure)

- Travel to Granada and take a horse-drawn carriage tour of the city.
- Visit the Chocolate Museum and enjoy a family-friendly chocolate-making workshop.
- Take a boat tour to the Islets of Granada and spot wildlife.

Day 7-9 (Ometepe Island and Nature Exploration)

- Take a ferry to Ometepe Island and engage in family-friendly hikes.
- Visit Charco Verde Nature Reserve and spot local wildlife.
- Enjoy family time in Ojo de Agua's natural springs and swimming areas.

Day 10-12 (Family Beach Retreat)

- Head to San Juan del Sur for a family-friendly beach vacation.
- Engage in beach activities like building sandcastles and swimming.
- Participate in surf lessons suitable for all ages.

Day 13-14 (Cultural Learning and Farewell)

- Return to Granada and visit a local school for cultural exchange.
- Enjoy a family cooking class to learn to prepare traditional Nicaraguan dishes.

- Depart with cherished memories of your family-friendly Nicaraguan adventure.

Whether you're an adventurer, a cultural enthusiast, or a family seeking quality time, Nicaragua's diverse landscapes and rich experiences cater to every traveler's interests. From volcanic hikes and cultural immersion to beach retreats and family fun, these sample itineraries provide a glimpse into the incredible journeys that await in Nicaragua. Customize and tailor these itineraries.

In conclusion, the "Nicaragua Travel Guide: The Complete Guide to Discover, Embark and Experience the Best of Nicaragua's Natural Beauty, Rich Culture and Vibrant History" encapsulates the essence of this captivating nation, offering a comprehensive journey through its landscapes, culture and adventures. From the colonial treasures of Granada to the pristine beaches of San Juan del Sur, the guide is a roadmap to unforgettable experience. I extend my heartfelt appreciation for joining me on this exploration and I hope this guide has enriched your understanding of Nicaragua's beauty, heritage and warmth of its people.

As you embark on your Nicaraguan journey, may your discoveries be as vast as the horizons that await you.

Printed in Great Britain
by Amazon

32054261R00096